Proud Past, Bright Future

Proud Past, Bright Future

ONE HUNDRED YEARS OF CANADIAN WOMEN'S HOCKEY

BRIAN McFARLANE

Stoddart

First published in 1994 by

Stoddart Publishing Co. Limited

34 Lesmill Road

Toronto, Canada

M3B 2T6

(416) 445-3333

CANADIAN CATALOGUING IN PUBLICATION DATA

McFarlane, Brian, 1931–
  Proud past, bright future: one hundred years of
Canadian women's hockey
Includes index.

ISBN 0-7737-2836-8

1. Hockey for women—Canada—History.
2. Hockey—Canada—History. I. Title.

GV848.4.C2X34 1994   796.962'082   C94-931834-5

Jacket Design: Brant Cowie/ArtPlus Limited
Printed in Canada

Stoddart Publishing gratefully acknowledges the support of the Canada Council, Ontario Ministry of Culture, Tourism, and Recreation, Ontario Arts Council, and Ontario Publishing Centre in the development of writing and publishing in Canada.

Title Page Photograph: Varsity women playing hockey at the University of Toronto in the early part of the 20th century.

(University of Toronto Archives)

To the pioneers — Isobel Stanley, Lulu Lemoine, Marian Hilliard, Bobbie Rosenfeld, Helen Nicholson Woltho, Margaret Topp Cater, Hilda Ranscombe, and the powerful Preston Rivulettes. To the superstars who aspire to world, Olympic, and possibly even professional championships in the future. To engaging enthusiasts like Samantha Holmes and lifelong contributors like Fran Rider. To the chroniclers past and present: Alexandrine Gibb, Myrtle Cook McGowan, Mary Ormsby, Lois Kalchman, and others. To the record number of young women who are registering for hockey and who play for the love of the game. And, yes, to Donna Munro (wherever she is and whatever her name may now be). And finally, to Norah, my all-star sister, to my granddaughters Samantha and Aubrey (may they grow up to play the game), and to those ageless sweethearts, Mississauga mayor Hazel McCallion, Mickey Walker, and Mabel Boyd.

Contents

Foreword   *ix*

Preface   *xv*

Prologue   1

1   *Long Skirts and Short Sticks   7*

2   *Taking the Game Seriously   45*

3   *Roar of the Rivulettes: The Thirties   77*

4   *When the Stickhandling Stopped: The Forties and Fifties   107*

5   *The Excitement Returns: The Sixties and Seventies   121*

6   *Better, Faster, Bolder: The Eighties   137*

7   *An Olympic Goal: The Nineties   151*

Epilogue   197

Index   *203*

Foreword

CANADIANS HAVE GROWN UP with hockey — it's an integral part of our society. In recent years the sport has been catching on in an increasing number of foreign countries. As the pages of this book unfold, readers will discover one of the best-kept secrets in Canadian history — women have enjoyed hockey, our great Canadian tradition, not just as spectators, but as avid, highly skilled players since before the beginning of the 20th century!

Most hockey enthusiasts and many others are now aware of the existence of female hockey. The 1992 announcement from the Barcelona Summer Olympics that women's hockey had been accepted by the International Olympic Committee as a full-medal sport, and then the subsequent acceptance by Japan to host the event in the 1998 Winter Olympics, brought instant credibility. Although exceptional competition exists in many sports at local, provincial, national, and international levels, participation in the Olympic games has a special reverence. Our athletes and our sport are now treated with the respect they deserve.

We owe our current success to the many great women and men who paved the way — both those who are recognized within this book and those who currently remain anonymous. The women who participated in the late 1800s and early 1900s must truly have loved the game since they faced such overwhelming public skepticism and hostility. It must have taken great courage to brave the outdoor rinks wearing skirts and, in later years, bloomers.

Despite substantial difficulties great stars did emerge to develop extraordinary skills even without proper training and support. And there were certainly gleamings of a

Team Canada '92 faces-off with the Central Ontario Women's Hockey League All-Stars in an exhibition game prior to the World Championship in Tampere, Finland. Canada won the game, but the All-Stars were no pushovers.
(Ontario Women's Hockey Association)

significant breakthrough in the 1930s as public credibility blossomed. However, the modern-day boom began in the 1960s, accelerated in the seventies, and sky-rocketed in the eighties, creating the momentum that will take the sport through the nineties and into the 21st century. In fact, the tremendous success of the eighties may not be duplicated in the history of any sport.

Again we owe a great deal to the tremendous dedication of people who were the driving forces behind teams, leagues, and tournaments. One contemporary stalwart hails from our smallest province, Prince Edward Island. Susan Dalziel, a skilled player, knowledgeable coach, and dedicated volunteer has demonstrated that individual effort can have exceptional impact.

Another person who has had a powerful influence is the highly respected mayor of Mississauga, Hazel McCallion. "Hurricane Hazel" leaves a positive impression because she cares deeply for people and has the determination and courage to work hard for her beliefs. A successful player in Quebec and an outstanding supporter of the Ontario Women's Hockey Association, Hazel is an inspiration to female hockey enthusiasts around the world.

Ontario has been a hotbed of women's hockey throughout the sport's history, and the formation of the OWHA in 1975 had exceptional results. The OWHA is the only organization of its kind in the world and it has been the catalyst for many developments.

The association administers all ages and levels of competition within the province, and its members are totally dedicated to the establishment, maintenance, and proactive development of female hockey locally, provincially, nationally, and internationally. By pooling efforts and working with supporters at all levels, strong house leagues and representative programs have been established. And substantial lobbying has also proven successful in securing the acceptance of female hockey in the Ontario Winter Games, the Canada Winter Games, the National Championship, the World Championship, and ultimately the Olympics.

Women's hockey has worked hard to establish a positive image that fosters exceptional skill levels, intelligent teamwork, and a high level of on-ice competition. This is accomplished within an atmosphere that ensures the "game" is kept in perspective, emphasizing fun, friendship, and fair play.

Our world-class athletes are exceptional people. It has become commonplace for individuals attending national selection camps or other high-level competitions to ask, "When do the players start hating one another? They're competing." Our response is simply to say that they won't. Our athletes truly love the game. They respect one another and recognize that the game requires many skills. They have a sincere appreciation for the sport as they've grown with it.

The success of female hockey is a fine example of the amazing accomplishments possible when everyone works toward a common goal. Provincial, national, and international borders have been ignored as female hockey enthusiasts joined together to attain "our" Olympic dream. Canada has led the way and has won three consecutive gold medals in World Championships sanctioned by the International Ice Hockey Federation. These have been great victories, but secondary to the collective advancements we've shared in the worldwide development and acceptance of female hockey.

We owe a great deal to so many. The existence of the OWHA was critical and has been made possible through the moral and financial support of the Ontario government. The OWHA has also received ongoing moral support from our brother organizations in Ontario — the Ontario Hockey Association, the Ottawa District Hockey Association, the Thunder Bay Amateur Hockey Association, the Metropolitan Toronto Hockey League, the Northern Ontario Hockey Association, the Ontario Hockey League, the Ontario Minor Hockey Association, the Minor Hockey Alliance of Ontario, and the Hockey Development Centre for Ontario. And, of course, nationally we have received support from the Canadian Amateur Hockey Association.

Some very special individuals have also had a major impact on our game. Brent Ladds, president of the OHA, is a key figure in hockey. He became a sincere believer and active supporter of female hockey at a critical time when many people felt females shouldn't even play the game. Brent opened many doors and has been a constant source of sound advice.

Gord Renwick, a Cambridge, Ontario, businessman, past chairman of the CAHA, and past vice president of the International Ice Hockey Federation, was instrumental in our acceptance into the 1998 Olympics in Japan. And Syl Apps assisted with our successful lobby into the Ontario Winter Games.

Professor Ed Ratushny has been a solid supporter of women's hockey, advising on many critical legal issues. *Toronto Star* freelance reporter Lois Kalchman is an active supporter and wrote numerous positive articles over many years.

Many NHL luminaries and broadcasters such as Ken Dryden, Darryl Sittler, Ron Ellis, Paul Henderson, and Ron MacLean, as well as Scotty Morrison, David Taylor, and others with the Hockey Hall of Fame, are active supporters of women's hockey, bringing us the same class and credibility they've brought to the male side of the game. The most important stars, however, are our players. With their enthusiasm, ability, and determination they have shown the world that girls and women do play hockey with exceptional skill. Perhaps the president of the CAHA, Murray Costello, put it best in an interview during the 1990 World Championship. He stated: "The women's game and how it's played, with artistry and finesse, could become the role model by which the men should really play the game."

I would like to extend my thanks to Nelson Doucet, Don Bastian, and Stoddart Publishing for their support of this book and also of female hockey. Sincere thanks also go out to Brian McFarlane for his tremendous support of women's hockey over many years. Brian is a first-class individual who sincerely loves the game of hockey and the people involved. We are honoured to have him write this unique book and share his knowledge with readers everywhere. And, finally, I sincerely congratulate the many individuals who have contributed to a very proud past. It is because of you that the youth of our country and the world have the opportunity to share in a very bright future.

FRAN RIDER
Executive Director
Ontario Women's Hockey Association

Preface

MY FIRST EXPERIENCE with women's hockey goes all the way back to the late forties and my high school days at Glebe Collegiate in Ottawa. Some of the girls decided to form a team there and I was asked to be the coach. The schedule consisted of two games, both against Lisgar Collegiate.

My sister Norah, two years younger than I (and today an award-winning novelist), tried out for the team along with two dozen other girls, and after one or two practice sessions on the outdoor rink, I was forced to make cuts. Unfortunately Norah was one of the girls who didn't make the final roster, and I have felt remorse and guilt about that decision ever since.

My debut as a coach in women's hockey was less than spectacular. Glebe lost both games to Lisgar and my players failed to score a goal. If Donna Munro, a dear little red-head, is reading this, she might be compelled to correct me. She might say, "Brian, we did score a goal. Remember how I was spun around in the second game, grabbed the puck, and scored on a breakaway?" Yes, Donna, I do remember that play. I recall it vividly, almost half a century later. I can see you now, squirming your way out of that pileup, grabbing the puck, and then skating *the wrong way* (were you a little dizzy, Donna?) and scoring on our astonished goaltender.

A more experienced coach might have anticipated such a calamity. Strangely enough, it never occurred to me to say anything to my charges about which direction a novice puckhandler should take.

Ladies' hockey team in Alberta, circa 1910.

(Edmonton Chamber of Commerce)

You will meet some Donna Munros in the pages ahead — girls who briefly tasted the joys of women's hockey. You will also meet others who are, like the members of Canada's World Championship teams, talented athletes and have honed their skills to near-perfection. And you will meet dedicated pros like Manon Rhéaume, remarkable "youngsters" like 75-year-old Mickey Walker and 72-year-old Mabel Boyd, strong-willed battlers like Cathy Phillips and Samantha Holmes, determined leaders like Fran Rider, Susan Dalziel, and Mississauga mayor Hazel McCallion.

You will be amazed, I am certain, at the splendid record of the Preston Rivulettes, a team that rivals the renowned Edmonton Grads of basketball fame for establishing a winning tradition like no other in Canadian women's sport. And you may be jolted by the story of a Cornwall lass who, in 1917, threw her skates aside and took a mysterious trip to New York in search of a drastic solution to a sexual identity crisis.

After writing more than 40 books dedicated to hockey in general, it has been a joy for me to explore the history of the women's game. I found the annals to be rich in fascinating facts, episodes, and anecdotes. My admiration goes out to the women who have struggled hard to find and maintain a place in the game. And that place is unique. Women have adopted a refreshingly different, more civilized attitude toward hockey than their male counterparts. Most are women first, hockey players second. The "win or else" ethic of the men's pro leagues is foreign to their nature. They appear to care about rivals, who are comrades and friends, not foes or enemies. They are rightfully proud of past efforts and obstacles overcome and they confidently look forward to a bright future.

I would like to extend a special thanks to Nancy Howden for her invaluable assistance in researching this book, to photographer Jane Sherk, and to my editor Michael Carroll. Unfortunately, in compiling these pages, certain players and teams may have been over-looked. I invite my readers to contact me if they feel a particular group or individual, past or present, has been neglected. Now that the initial foray has been made into the heritage of women's hockey, other historians will follow (hopefully they will be women), and to them we will leave additional information and fresh areas to explore.

I sincerely hope the thousands of young women now involved in hockey discover the same peculiar feeling for the game that national team member Sue Scherer described for me. Her words struck a nerve because it is the same feeling I have experienced myself for as far back as I can remember:

> It comes from a little bubble inside me somewhere. So that every time I put on my skates there's this little bubble and it says I've got to play. I've got to play hockey! It's simply a feeling that catches hold of you and won't go away. I don't think I'll ever lose it.

BRIAN MCFARLANE
Toronto

Prologue

THEY DIDN'T EXPECT IT, really they didn't. Not this much and not this soon. But ever since Ottawa in 1990, and the glorious moments when Canada's pink-jerseyed skaters captured the World Championship of women's hockey before a nationwide television audience, the spotlight has been on women in hockey. That's when women players began to emerge from the shadow of their male counterparts. That's when they received the recognition, admiration, acceptance, and attention they so richly deserved.

These energetic women who don blades and participate in one of the world's fastest growing team games are not called gals, girls, females, or even ladies — they are simply women. And when they lug that equipment bag to the rink and suit up for a scrimmage or a game, they become women players — hockey players. What they didn't expect, not this soon, was full and total acceptance into the world of hockey, a domain that (surely no one will argue) has been a male-dominated one since long before that bearded Englishman Lord Stanley, a sports-minded governor general from another century, shelled out $50 to purchase a cup for the game.

Now, in the 1990s, 100 years after a few pioneer women laced on skates in the late 1800s and picked up hand-me-down sticks, they have arrived in vast numbers and with the promise of many more to come. They are women of all ages, sizes, and nationalities and they have one obvious thing in common — a zest for the game. They love to play. They are a presence in hockey, a huge presence, and they have finally erased the old perception, lodged in the minds of men, that women should be at home knitting, cooking, or burping babies, not skating

Windsor, Nova Scotia, claims to be the birthplace of men's hockey in Canada. Many of the town's women's teams were highly rated. In the early thirties Dot Chisholm of Windsor (wearing the cloche hat next to the team manager) was one of the best female players in the country.

(Howard Dill Collection)

1

around some rock-hard ice surface on sharp steel runners, risking their looks and their limbs in a harsh body-contact sport.

This perception has not been an easy one to eradicate. After all, a century-old bias will not likely change if there is no change. And in the past 10 years women in hockey have been doing a lot of changing. They pushed for and ultimately won recognition from the male-dominated hierarchy of the sport. They conducted one unofficial world tournament in North York and Mississauga, Ontario, in 1987. They conducted three official Women's World Hockey Championships (sanctioned by the International Ice Hockey Federation), the first in 1990, a second in 1992, and a third in April 1994 in Lake Placid, New York. And they succeeded in having their sport added to the list of events at the 1998 Winter Olympics in Nagano, Japan — a major triumph.

What's more, three of their gender — Manon Rhéaume, Kelly Dyer, and Erin Whitten — all goaltenders, created astonishing news by proving they could play on a par with men and become winners in professional hockey.

A century of women pursuing hockey pucks in Canada has produced many personal and team accomplishments. It was during the 1930s that a team from Preston, Ontario, elevated the game to unheard-of heights, setting standards for others to emulate. Over a decade of play the slick-passing, hard-shooting Preston Rivulettes glued themselves to the championship trophy, baby-sitting the national women's title from 1930 to 1939 and

carving a prestigious 348–2 won-loss record into Canadian hockey history. This dynasty helped to jump-start women's hockey as a form of competition. The game was still fun, it was still recreation, but it was hockey played for keeps . . . by women.

The Rivulettes' record clamours for attention, especially in Canada where women who excel in sports are dear to our hearts, for example, Barbara Ann Scott, Silken Laumann, and Myriam Bédard. But who has ever heard of the Preston Rivulettes? The NHL? Not likely. The Hockey Hall of Fame? Perhaps. Anyone under 50? Not a chance.

Just as it has been a tradition to keep women — most of them — in the family kitchen over the past 100 years, it has been a tradition to keep the achievements of those who venture onto ice with sticks and gloves hidden in the shadows of male idols — superstars like Howie Morenz, Gordie Howe, and Wayne Gretzky, and super teams like the Montreal Canadiens and the Toronto Maple Leafs.

An exchange between a young sportswriter and his editor in the 1930s might have gone something like this:

Reporter: Boss, I hear the Preston Rivulettes girls' team has a record of something like 200–0. Want me to do a little story on their success for the next edition?

Editor: Are you kiddin' me? With everybody talking about the playoff battle between the Leafs and the Habs, I've got no space for that. Besides, who in hell are the Preston Rivulettes? A girls' team, you say? Girls can't play hockey. Everyone knows that. Get outta here.

"BREAK THE ICE . . . start a new tradition," proclaimed the Canadian Amateur Hockey Association in 1983. So far it has taken more than 100 years for the old tradition of men's hockey to move aside grudgingly in order that women may share ice space with them. At long last the doors to countless arenas have flown open to women with pucks and payment for ice time.

3

Today more than 20,000 Canadian girls and women sign up each winter to play hockey, many with visions of 1990s star Manon Rhéaume dancing in their heads. Others dream of participating in national championships or basking in Olympic glory. Most just don their skates and play for the sheer joy of it.

Many of Canada's veteran women stars have had to be patient. The chance to compete as Olympians is a special challenge they thought would never come. They came so close to being invited to Lillehammer and now they must show more patience and pray their hockey legs will still be strong in 1998 — for Nagano.

Even though the International Ice Hockey Federation and the Norwegian Ice Hockey Federation backed the bid for women's hockey to be included in the 1994 Olympic Games, the Lillehammer Olympic Organizing Committee rejected the application, citing a million-dollar price tag as the major obstacle.

When was the first-ever women's hockey match played? Diligent research has produced the first newspaper account of a game played in Ottawa in 1891, one year prior to a game played in Barrie, Ontario, which for years has been widely publicized as the birthplace of women's hockey. It is certain the women who attended Lord and Lady Stanley's skating parties held on the Rideau Hall rink in the 1880s played mixed games of shinny on a large rink situated on the grounds.

Hockey's popularity among women has shown unparalleled growth with an explosion of recent

Team Canada members Stacy Wilson (left), Manon Rhéaume, and Margot Verlaan.
(Ontario Women's Hockey Association)

interest becoming the developing story of the nineties. The raw numbers of players and fans turning out, plus the snowballing coverage by the media, assures a very bright future.

It has been an arduous journey to this point, but we were warned it wouldn't be easy. Writing in the *Toronto Daily Star* on March 23, 1934, 60 years ago, Alexandrine Gibb said: "Women's hockey is just blossoming out as a Canadian-wide contest. It is too much to believe that everything will run along smoothly at first. Rough ice is bound to be met. Conditions unexpected and unethical will also face the hockey pioneers. . . ."

More than 100 years after a handful of pioneer players made the "first" all-female hockey match an important part of women's hockey history, an equally dedicated band reaches out toward that famous flame and those five fascinating rings . . . and another "first" — an Olympic hockey championship.

1

Long Skirts and Short Sticks

The earliest known photograph of women playing at Rideau Hall in Ottawa, circa 1890. Isobel Stanley, Lord Stanley's daughter, is in white.

(National Archives of Canada)

LORD STANLEY OF PRESTON, Canada's sixth governor general, is the only honoured member of the Hockey Hall of Fame who was never a player of note, never a coach, a referee, a team owner, or an executive. He was recalled to England in 1893 after serving as Her Majesty's representative in Canada. As a result, he was denied the pleasure of witnessing even a single playoff game for the great trophy that bears his name — the Stanley Cup.

There is no doubt Lord Stanley thoroughly enjoyed the 1890s brand of hockey that was played during his term in Ottawa. So did his hockey-playing sons and his two daughters. When his term was almost up, they badgered him to donate something of a lasting nature to the game. His Excellency conceived the idea of a trophy, a challenge trophy, in the form of a silver bowl worth about $50, one that would be captured each year by the amateur hockey champions of Canada.

We all know that his modest donation soon became one of the most famous trophies in the realm of sport, an everlasting symbol of hockey supremacy. A full century after his

Lord Stanley provided the ice for women's games at Rideau Hall long before he donated the Stanley Cup to hockey.
(National Archives of Canada)

departure for England — because of his gift — the name Stanley remains as familiar to all Canadians as any prime minister.

But recent research into Lord Stanley's five happy years in residence at Government House in Ottawa leads us to conclude that the Stanley Cup wasn't his only — or his first — contribution to hockey. There is firm evidence that he and Lady Stanley played a significant role in the development and growth of women's hockey — simply by creating an environment in which the game could be enjoyed in a casual manner by men and women alike.

Lord Stanley might be called an 1890s version of Canada's most famous backyard rink builder — Walter Gretzky. He sought a suitable place for a rink of his own, where he and Lady Stanley, their sons and daughters, and family friends could experience the joys of skating and the thrills of hockey. Early in his term and under his supervision a large lawn on the grounds of Rideau Hall was hosed down by members of his staff (Walter Gretzky did it himself), and frequent floodings soon turned the flattened grass into a gleaming, icy, winter-long playground.

By then the Stanleys were already hooked on hockey. They had arrived in Ottawa from London, England, in 1888, and shortly thereafter attended the annual Winter Carnival in Montreal. There they witnessed a thrilling hockey match between the Montreal Vics and the Montreal Amateur Athletic Association, and became instant fans of the game.

As an avid sportsman and energetic 48-year-old father of 10 — eight sons and two daughters — it was natural that His Excellency would want to strap on skates and try the game himself. And he did — once he had supervised the flooding of his mammoth outdoor rink. He encouraged all of his family members, including Lady Stanley, to do likewise. The lure of that smooth sheet of ice, flooded daily by a caretaker, must have been irresistible to the Stanley clan. It even brought Lord Stanley out on the Sabbath which, in those Victorian times, was almost as sinful as playing cards or rolling dice on the seventh day.

Then, as now, practice makes perfect, and soon most of the Stanleys — their high-society friends and staff members at Government House — became accomplished skaters and hockey players. Three of the Stanley sons — Edward, Algernon, and Arthur — became so skilled with stick and puck that they formed a team named the Rebels and played exhibition games in several Ontario centres, including Toronto.

Both of Lord Stanley's daughters became rabid hockey fans. Daughter Isobel (who later became Lady Isobel Gathorne-Hardy) was one of the first woman hockey players in Canada. She played for a Government House team that was matched against the Rideau ladies. It is conceivable that this was the first women's hockey game in history, played on the rink at Government House early in 1889.

There is photographic evidence to support this claim. A tiny snapshot found in the Gathorne-Hardy collection at the National Archives in Ottawa, when enlarged, reveals several women wearing long skirts and holding short hockey sticks on the ice at Rideau Hall. Isobel is dressed in white. It is also quite possible the male figure in the photo is Lord Stanley himself. This unique photo is the earliest known image on film of women involved in a game of hockey. It is also one of the very few (if not the only) "action" shots from that era.

In 1893, when Lord Stanley's term expired and he and his family returned to England, he was instrumental in introducing hockey to British society. Five of the Stanleys challenged a Buckingham Palace team to a game played on the grounds of the palace. Among the palace skaters was the Prince of Wales (later King Edward VII) and the Duke of York (who became King George V).

Back in Canada Lord Stanley's legacy touched sports-minded Canadians from coast to coast. His little Stanley Cup became the most sought-after trophy in Canadian history. Hockey men were soon spending fortunes in feverish efforts to capture it.

And women? The ladies photographed on the ice at Government House had already opened the door. If high-society women like the refined Lady Isobel and her cultured friends could enjoy the pleasures of hockey, then why couldn't any woman with a pair of skates and a borrowed stick try her hand at the game? And thousands did.

Women in Wimbledon Park, England, playing hockey with sticks and a ball in January 1893. (National Archives of Canada)

10

During the early 1900s, and even before, women's teams were organized throughout most of the Canadian provinces — and as far away as Dawson City in the Yukon. During the Klondike gold rush — that mad scramble for riches that lured thousands of adventurous young men and women to Dawson City at the turn of the century — hockey fever was such that an impressive indoor arena was soon constructed in that bustling mining town. The

Dawsons versus Victorias. Game played in the new Dawson City Arena in 1904.

(Glenbow Archives, Calgary)

games between local teams were well attended — even more so when the women players took to the ice. Men jammed the balcony above the ice surface — some of them cheering their lady friends through megaphones — and the level of play was said to be quite high.

The women were quite content to play among themselves. It was foolish to think of challenging teams in far-off Edmonton or any other place where women were taking up the game. Let the bold men of Dawson seek outside challenges if they wished — and they did. In 1904 a handful of male players formed the Nuggets and challenged the famous Ottawa Silver Seven for the Stanley Cup. The saga of their 4,000-mile-plus journey to Ottawa by bicycle, dogsled, steamship, and train — not to mention covering the first 350 miles to Whitehorse on foot — has been well chronicled and is one of the great adventure stories in sports. After 23 days on the road, sea, and rails, with no opportunity to skate or practise, the Dawson City Nuggets reached Ottawa where they were humiliated by scores of 9–2 and 23–2.

Despite allowing a record-high 32 goals in the two games, Albert Forrest, Dawson City's 17-year-old netminder, was praised by the Ottawa sportswriters. "Forrest was sensational," one of them wrote. "Without him the score would have been double what it was." Young Forrest wasn't the only hockey player in his family. Years later sister Evelyn would star for the Laval University team.

Early in the new century women's teams sprouted up in places large and small. Arenas for them to play in were under construction everywhere, although outdoor play was the norm. In the West, Edmonton, Calgary, Banff, Medicine Hat, Okotoks, Vulcan, and Vancouver spoke proudly of their women's teams. A photo of an unidentified women's team in western Canada, taken in 1896, is one of the earliest that painstaking research has been able to uncover.

By then the game was firmly established in eastern centres such as Montreal, Quebec City, Saint John, Fredericton, Moncton, Ottawa, Kingston, and Toronto. In the Maritimes and other places the men tried hard to keep the game to themselves. And it was largely played by men who belonged to the proper social and athletic clubs. Blue-collar workers, farmers, and dock-hands weren't welcome no matter how skilled they were. The ladies of the men who played — also members of the upper social set — insisted on lacing up their skates and playing, too. Their games and practices weren't open to the public, and it was reported that they played a snappy brand of hockey. In his book *Saint John: A Sporting Tradition*, Brian Flood quotes a *Sun* reporter of the era: "Some of the women hockey players are very swift skaters and they can dodge with the puck to equal some of the best gentlemen players."

The Saint John women often travelled to Moncton and Fredericton where they would compete in lively games against women who shared their love for the sport. The competing

teams would skate out wearing long linen skirts. Their sweaters might have a crest, emblem, or large letter of the alphabet stitched loosely across the front — for identification purposes.

There is evidence that women's teams were formed in many communities across Canada during this era. In winter the college girls at McGill University in Montreal had been playing games of hockey once or twice weekly since 1894. They were granted four hours of ice time per week on the indoor rink providing three men were on duty to guard the entrances. No male students were allowed to become involved and the players had to be comfortably and warmly dressed. In time the women objected to these conditions, and when another arena was erected behind Royal Victoria College, they organized interclass games in the new rink. The referee for these matches generally ignored any infractions and blew his whistle three times — to begin play, to signal halftime, and to end the contest.

An early Montreal ladies' hockey team, one of many to spring up in Quebec at the beginning of the 20th century.
(Author's Collection)

It was more difficult for the women at Queen's to become involved. A team of Queen's women, calling themselves the Love-Me-Littles (named because their on-ice antics had university officials shaking their heads in disapproval), boldly challenged the male members of the varsity team to a scrimmage. This brazen behaviour earned them a strongly worded rebuke from the archbishop of the university.

Undaunted, the following year they began charging admission to their games, profiting by as much as $50 per contest. Hundreds came to see them play, and they received many compliments for their clever stickhandling, passing, and shooting.

In 1900 the first known women's league was formed in La Belle Province. As someone said: "It is as natural for Quebec girls to skate as it is for other women to walk." Three teams from Montreal were joined by a team from Trois-Rivières and one from Quebec City. Obviously the shy stickhandlers from Trois-Rivières had shed their inhibitions and were now willing to display their skills in public. Until 1900 anyone wishing to see a member of this team in action — skirt bunched around her ankles, stick resting against rubber and poised to shoot — was out of luck. "No spectators allowed" was a strictly enforced rule whenever the Trois-Rivières ladies took to the ice. Only the referee and a pair of goal judges — three males — were permitted to watch them perform. Perhaps the players in that community were concerned about the embarrassment of falling down and having skirts fly up. One newspaper account suggested that young women took up the game merely to stay à la mode and be part of the hockey rage that was beginning to sweep the nation.

"The Trois-Rivières ladies do not wish to be left behind in healthy exercise on ice and are taking advantage of the splendid covered rink built here," said a team spokesman. She might have added: "We also wish to do so in private."

This desire for anonymity was not uncommon. Many women's teams of that era preferred to hold games and practices behind closed doors. No men allowed. Because women players generally were not competing for fame and glory — like their male counterparts who hungered for Stanley Cup titles and lesser awards — when women did display their skills on ice in public, their games were not well publicized or promoted. As a result, few spectators attended.

In Stratford, Ontario, where a large arena was constructed in the late 19th century, women donned skates, took up sticks, and began to play the game as early as 1895. But like their counterparts in Trois-Rivières, they were shy maidens and men were strictly forbidden from entering the premises when the women were at play. The names of the players involved were never published and there was total agreement that no photographs of them would ever be taken. Several years passed before they decided there was no harm in playing in public and by 1917 the Stratford ladies had an enviable record — only one loss in two seasons of play.

Western women were not about to let their eastern sisters get too much of a head start in the game. Some even argued that the East was taking too much credit for inventing the game. According to the April 1984 edition of *The Alberta Report*, "the first women's team in Canada was formed in Medicine Hat, Alberta, in 1893," and thus Alberta "holds the distinction of being the birthplace of organized women's hockey. The first provincial tournament took place 13 years later when a six-team league competed in Banff." While Alberta women are applauded for being quick off the mark, the preceding claim is a false one. The Medicine Hat girls lagged well behind the women from Ontario.

By 1900 a small group of Ottawa ladies had already carved a sizable niche for themselves among the game's pioneers. They had been accustomed to playing with sticks and a puck for a decade. The first written account of a game between two unnamed women's teams appeared in the *Ottawa Citizen* on February 11, 1891. It was quite brief:

A ladies hockey match was played at the Rideau rink yesterday between teams as follows: No. 1: Miss MacIntosh, Captain; Miss Wise, Munro, Ritchie, Camby, Jones, White. No. 2: Miss H. Wise, Captain; Miss MacIntosh, Ritchie, McClymont, Burrows and Mrs. Gordon. Number two team won by two goals to none.

Research has failed to turn up a newspaper report of a women's hockey game predating the above match in Ottawa.

The above item also disproves another claim, sanctioned by women's hockey groups for many years, that Barrie, Ontario, deserves recognition as the site of the first organized game of women's hockey, a match played there in 1892. It is hoped that Barrie's city fathers have not yet proudly erected highway signs proclaiming this important historical fact.

A thorough perusal of the *Northern Advance*, which covered Barrie's sports events quite well in that era, revealed but one description of a woman's hockey match played in that community in 1892. It took place in mid-February before 400 fans and it was not a bona fide match between women but a frivolous charade with women playing men dressed as women. Still, it was fun.

By 1896 the newspapers were paying a little more attention to women on ice. In Kingston, Ontario, Queen's students on the distaff side were reported to be quite excited about hockey. The Morning Glories of Queen's defeated the Black and Blues of the ladies college in a game. Perhaps it was the surprising amount of interest in the match that led to increased newspaper coverage. In a return contest, played before 1,200 spectators, the Black and Blues squared the series.

During the 1896 season, a game witnessed "by many spectators" was played in Smiths Falls, Ontario. The Alpha Ladies Club of Ottawa defeated the Smiths Falls girls by a score of 4–2. Both teams received great applause when they made their appearance. The Ottawa girls wore white jerseys, which had the letter *A* worked in red on the front. Their red skirts and white tam-o'-shanters made the local girls, dressed in blue, look drab by comparison.

Fresh from their triumph in Smiths Falls, the Alpha ladies were invited to play at Government House on March 17, 1896. The *Ottawa Citizen* gave the match a considerable amount of attention:

That the Alpha and Rideau Ladies Hockey teams can play the game was well demonstrated at the Rideau rink last night when they met in a friendly match. Both teams played grandly and surprised hundreds of the sterner sex who went to the match expecting to see many ludicrous scenes and have many good laughs. Indeed, before they were there very long, their sympathies and admiration had gone out to the teams. The men became wildly enthusiastic. The match ended in a tie, the score being one to one. What the Rideau team lacked as a whole was made up for by the good individual playing of Mrs. Smith and Miss Lulu Lemoine, especially the latter who was the best player on the ice.

Miss Lemoine continued to excel at the game and played for several years. In 1899, in another of the many games played on the Government House rink, according to the *Ottawa Citizen*, her skills were matched by Lady Minto, wife of the governor general:

The game of hockey has converted the Government House party and Ottawa's 400 from enthusiastic admirers to participants. Mixed teams, drawing their members from the above circles, tried conclusions with the puck and stick on Rideau rink ice on Saturday afternoon. At the call of time the score stood 7 to 6 in favour of the Government House team, showing that her Majesty's representatives take to hockey as kindly and successfully as they do to other Canadian institutions. The game furnished much amusement and some skillful play.

The ladies on both sides played with a vim quite foreign to their natures. Lady Minto (who once broke her leg while skating) played at cover point and the manner in which she went up the ice was a revelation to the other players. The playing of Miss Lulu Lemoine was particularly good, her bodychecking and dodging being the feature of the match. Lady Sibel between the flags stopped many difficult shots and repeatedly saved her team. Lady Elliot's position was point and the manner in which she lifted the puck evoked loud applause.

Among the onlookers was Mr. George Meagher, the champion figure skater of the world, who said, "I have seen all the best skaters of the world and I consider Her Excellency, the Countess of Minto, to be the peer of them all. Lady Minto has all the qualifications of the finished expert on skates, which are grace, suppleness and strength."

A few months later Lord and Lady Minto's love of skating led to tragic consequences and considerable damage to Lord Minto's reputation. Among other things, His Excellency was branded as "reckless, irresponsible and ignorant of the dangers involved in skating on thin ice."

In 1901 an early winter made for ideal skating conditions on the Ottawa River. Old-timers warned residents of the danger of thin ice, but many, including Lord and Lady Minto (and star player Lulu Lemoine), ignored the warnings. One day the governor general, leading a party of a dozen skaters, left the Government House dock and skated downriver. An hour later a second group of skaters followed. Among the latter was Henry Harper, 29-year-old assistant deputy minister of labour and roommate of William Lyon Mackenzie King, future prime minister of Canada.

Both skating parties travelled several miles downstream, and it was dark when they headed back. Five members of Lord Minto's group, including Miss Lemoine, crashed through the thin ice and had to swim for their lives. When they were finally able to crawl from the hole in the ice, they were faced with the daunting challenge of skating eight miles back to Government House.

Night closed in and it became impossible for the second group to distinguish between thick ice and thin. Suddenly two of them — Alex Creelman and his lady friend May Blair (daughter of a cabinet minister) — plunged through the ice into deep water. While a third

An Owen Sound, Ontario, team in the late 1890s.
(Saskatoon Public Library Local History Room)

member of the party dashed off to seek help, Henry Harper, crawling along the ice on his stomach, attempted to pull Miss Blair from the river. But each time he reached out the ice cracked ominously under the weight of his body. Author Sandra Gwyn, writing of the tragedy in *The Private Capital*, described what followed:

> Then Harper stood up and threw off his gauntlets. "For God's sake, Harper, don't come in too," shouted Creelman. Harper plunged into the water and swam towards Bessie. His last words, reported by Creelman, were, "What else can I do?" Even before Harper had managed to reach Bessie, the two were pulled under the ice by the current.

Creelman was able to cling to the ice for some time, and eventually two stragglers in the skating party came along and were able to pull him to safety.

The Ottawa newspapers carried front-page articles about the drownings, but Lord Minto was a man of influence. As a result, little mention was made of his reckless actions in leading the skaters into danger, although it was talked of in everyday conversation. Nor did the papers focus on the fact that several members of Lord Minto's party had narrowly escaped death when they crashed through the ice. No inquest was held.

Lady Minto once submitted her thoughts on skating to *The Badminton Magazine.* She wrote: "The Canadian boy can skate as soon as he can walk. It matters nothing to him if he skates on ice, or snow on the frozen sidewalk or road; it becomes second nature; his balance is perfect and his confidence complete." It is hard to believe Lady Minto ignored Canadian girls in her discourse, for, as author Anson Card put it in 1904, "the proficiency on ice of some of these dear little girls is nothing short of marvellous. They remind one of swallows on the wing, so easy they flit about over the ice and seem never to tire."

Hockey teams for women were not only blossoming in Ontario, but in the other provinces, as well. The *Cape Breton Post* was advertising for players because "there are several lady hockeyists in town who are desirous of organizing teams." On February 3, 1905, the Alpha women's team of Summerside, Prince Edward Island, won the first-ever game played between Summerside and Charlottetown. A ladies' hockey club was formed in Regina in 1896, and two years later there were women's teams in Vancouver.

Americans were also showing interest. In 1899 the *Ottawa Citizen* wrote of a game between two teams made up of women for the Ice Palace in Philadelphia where they would play on artificial ice.

Prairie women learned to play using tree limbs for sticks.

(Saskatchewan Archives Board)

In Guelph, Ontario, there was even talk of charging admission to see the girls perform. And the *Ottawa Citizen* wrote of a confident Ottawa Valley team that issued a nationwide challenge: "The fair creatures of Carleton Place have a hockey team and are open for challengers from any other ladies seven in Canada."

As early as 1900, Quebec society women engaged themselves in the new pastime in an effort to raise money for charity. On January 25, 1900, the following appeared in the *Toronto Star:*

> The organization from which the teams were picked is called the Quebec Ladies Hockey Club, and the match was an exhibition one, given in aid of the Soldier's Wives League. Of course there was a large crowd present for aside from the nature of the match, an appeal for that fund always calls forth a hearty reponse. But people wanted to see how women would play hockey and a most agreeable surprise they got, for the game was well-played and the match was an exciting one. The league fund will be richer by $125 for this scheme for its benefit. The players all wore ordinary skating skirts, and some of them, notably Miss Edith White, displayed much skill. The match was played in three halves, or rather thirds, of about a quarter of an hour each. It is probable that other matches will be played before the winter is over; at any rate, the interest in the sport is unflagging.

In Saskatchewan, before the old century expired, hockey was becoming just as popular with women as it was with men. Young women, then as now, kept a keen eye on the eligible young men in the community and made it a point to follow their athletic pursuits. But when the hockey craze swept across the frozen sloughs and streams of the West, with players in overalls hacking off tree limbs for sticks and using horse droppings or the knot from a knothole for a puck, women desired to be more than spectators. There was more fun in the playing. And the menfolk had good reason for wanting them to play — often there simply weren't enough male skaters around to make up a decent game of shinny.

When there weren't enough men
to ice a team for shinny in Viking,
Alberta, women were recruited.

(Saskatchewan Archives Board)

The women waded in. With their long skirts, heavy turtleneck sweaters, and tree branch sticks, they skated right into the thick of the scrimmages. And they remained there for the next 100 years.

Miss Annie McIntyre, reputed to be one of the fastest skaters in the province, helped organize Saskatchewan's first women's hockey team in 1896. Within a decade, leagues for female players were in vogue in places such as North and South Battleford, where games were played indoors and out. Teams travelled by horse and cutter to the games, and because no bridges as yet connected the two Battlefords, the horses clip-clopped over the frozen river while the players huddled under heavy blankets to keep warm.

Hockey historian Joe Zeman, in *88 Years of Puck Chasing in Saskatchewan*, recalls meeting Miss Walls, goaltender on one of those Battleford teams. Miss Walls, an art teacher in

Maritime Mothers Made Chest Protectors

Shortly after the turn of the century, when women goalies began worrying about protecting themselves from opponents' shots, it was easy to borrow shinpads and gloves from male players. But protection for the chest — essential for women and unimportant to men — was another matter. Marie Hiscock, writing in the Charlottetown Journal Pioneer in 1948, described how Maritime mothers protected their goalie daughters by using long needles and nimble fingers, plus a little feminine ingenuity.

They made homemade chest pads by sewing together layers of unbleached cotton and fashioning several long pockets with open tops across the front. Sawdust, easily acquired from any backyard or workshop in those days, was used to fill in the pockets and then was packed down until it was an inch or two thick.

Finally the top of the pocket — the flap — was closed and sewn tight to prevent the sawdust from spilling out and to keep the pad as firm as possible. Total cost — perhaps 15 cents.

Saskatoon in the thirties, called student Zeman into her office one day to ask him why he had come to class without his tie. "If I'd known she was a hockey player in her youth," Zeman writes, "we wouldn't have been talking neckties." Zeman notes that women's hockey was played at the University of Saskatchewan as early as 1913, with organized high school teams taking to the ice a couple of years later.

Creative team nicknames became an attractive feature of Prairie hockey. Who wouldn't be proud to wear the colours of the Arena Icebergs, the Civil Service Snowflakes, the Biggar Floradoras, the Dundurn Amazons, the Moose Jaw Wildcats, the Meadow Lake Golden Girls, or the Saskatchewan Prairie Lilies? There was even a team from Indian Head with the unflattering name of Old Hens.

In *One Hundred — Not Out*, Henry Roxborough explores the world of women in sport in the 1890s, when women embraced figure skating, tennis, baseball, and curling. In 1891 in Regina at least 60 women familiar with firearms entered a rifle-shooting competition. During the same decade, women began invading hockey rinks and were soon displaying skills that won the admiration of the male players.

Roxborough tells of one enterprising McGill player who, in 1894, developed a skill that until then was unknown in the game. After chasing a puck at full speed, she trapped it between her skates and let her momentum carry player and puck down the ice. When her speed slackened, she used her stick like a barge pole to propel herself toward the goal. As she neared the goal, she released the puck from between her feet and gave it a solid whack with her stick, sending it toward the net. Her enterprising tactic resulted in three goals during one game, all in the first half. In the second half an opponent had seen quite enough of the three-goal scorer's novel form of offence. She lifted her stick and delivered a two-hander to the puck carrier's ankles, freeing the puck and sending the girl carrying it crashing to the ice, howling in pain. The stick swinger, a professor's daughter who showed no remorse, was suspended for the rest of the season.

Perhaps it is worth noting that when a player put the puck in the net in one of these early-day matches, the result was often described as a "game." A game was the period of time between scores, hence the word *game* was often employed to mean goal.

In most communities, newspapers of the day devoted little attention to sports (much less than a page in the majority of instances) and reporters in the early 1900s didn't know how to handle this new development of women on the ice. On February 15, 1902, in the *Toronto Star*, what began as a routine account of a Belleville–Kingston game turned into a bizarre commentary on the players' ages and weights — prose that would never appear in today's mainstream publications:

The lady hockey players of Belleville had a most enjoyable time last night when the Scorchers met a team from Kingston, who called themselves the Aerials. The Kingston ladies were better stickhandlers than their opponents and the game ended: Aerials 5, Scorchers 0. But the score is no indication of the merits of the two teams. The Kingston maidens, it must be admitted, were good skaters and stickhandlers, but when their ages and weight are taken into consideration, it is no wonder they won the game. The Kingston team was composed of women, many of them old enough to be the mothers of some of the Belleville girls, but then they cannot help getting old.

The match had an interesting twist — exhaustion forced Belleville's star forward, Marjorie Hamilton, to leave the ice. She had to be assisted to the dressing room after playing a stellar game for the Scorchers.

Other hockey reports — some quite amusing — indicate that bodychecking was frowned upon by women's hockey officials. After a ladies' match in 1905, the reporter wrote: "Miss Janet Allen was ruled off for one minute for being a bad girl. She checked one of the Richview girls real hard."

Although bodychecking and rough play were frowned upon in women's play during those early years, it was impossible to keep tempers entirely under control — on and off the ice. This account appeared in a Toronto newspaper shortly after the turn of the century:

> The Whitby ladies defeated Oshawa last night by a score of 2–1. The visitors scored the winning goal just as the whistle blew for time. The referee did not hear the whistle and allowed the goal. Some of the spectators protested in vigorous fashion, leaping onto the ice and assaulting the referee.

After witnessing girls at play in another game, the reporter wrote: "Some of the girls are fast enough. Others are slow enough to make successful pallbearers."

A myth evolved that pioneer women players were "terribly genteel." Jean Walker played in goal for St. Hilda's College at the University of Toronto in 1904 and 1905. She told *Globe and Mail* reporter Jean Sharp in 1966 that it wasn't so. In fact, sometimes it was quite the opposite. However, if she and her teammates' style of play was somewhat unladylike back then, nobody seemed to care.

Walker's long skirt was just as effective in stopping blistering shots on goal as shinpads, she maintained. She said she didn't really need leg padding. She just ducked a bit and the long woollen skirt kept the puck from bruising an ankle. Some women goalies frustrated opposing shooters by sewing buckshot pellets into the hem of their skirts. The additional weight kept the skirts down at ice level. Opponents with weak shots could barely move the weighted skirt. It was like shooting into the side of a pegged-down tent.

Walker and her teammates wore ankle-length dark skirts, high-necked blouses, blue-trimmed V-neck sweaters, and knitted toques with tassels. The class colours, blue and silver, were sewn into the SHC insignia knitted in each pullover for the St. Hilda's College team.

"There was no organized physical education back then," Walker recalled. "Male college players acted as coaches. And there weren't many of us — only 14 girls in our class. If you didn't go out for a team, why, there wasn't one."

The attitude and actions of some of the college girls angered those who were determined to take the game seriously. Newspaper accounts of certain games made the competitors look ridiculous. As a result, the women's game suffered — dismissed as frivolous entertainment, good for a chuckle or two and little more. If the girls themselves chose to make a travesty or a burlesque of the game by their actions on the ice, they could hardly blame the rinkside reporters who lampooned them. The following paragraphs are extracted from an account of a game between Victoria College students in Toronto in 1901:

The game started without a referee, but the players refused to abide by the OHA rules and regulations, so a husky young college player was pressed into service. "Oh, say! I wasn't ready," said the Picture Hats' centre forward when her opponent took the puck from her on the face-off. The puck was brought back.

During the next attack on goal, the Picture Hats' point player was knocked down in front of the goal. This jar disarranged her hat and she calmly sat on the ice, removed her hat pins, rearranged her tresses, and replaced the hat. Down the ice came a Tam with the puck.

"Is my hat on straight?" asked the young lady on the ice when the player with the puck tried to lift the disc through the goal. Being assured on this point, she scrambled to her feet and rushed it down to the other end.

"Oh, my goodness, excuse me, Clarence!" exclaimed the Tams' cover point, hastily breaking up a tete-a-tete with a young man on the fence and rushed across the ice to defend the threatened goal.

"Half time, Mr. Referee," gasped a young woman, very much out of breath and throwing her arms around a convenient fence post. The game had progressed only five minutes. Mr. Referee tried to explain this, but the young lady said she was out of breath and that settled it.

When the game started again, the Picture Hats made a determined effort to even up the score, but their big hats persisted in sliding to one side at critical moments and the rude Tams absconded with the puck while their opponents were rearranging their refractory headgear.

Finally, Miss Alice, a Picture Hat forward, solved the problem by sitting on the puck while she manipulated hatpins. Tired players sat around in picturesque attitudes on the ice, and the referee called the game when the only players left standing were the goalkeepers and the young woman who was whispering sweet nothings to dear Clarence at the end of the rink.

With the exception of the absurd behaviour of the players above, most women were keen to learn the skills of the game and to play it properly. If a bloody nose resulted from overly aggressive play, so be it. Perhaps the spunk and spirit they displayed stemmed from their mothers and grandmothers, for upon the strong shoulders of pioneer women fell some awesome responsibilities. They maintained a home under primitive and arduous conditions, often in desolate parts of the country. They nursed babies, raised large families, and made all of the family clothes by means of an old-time spinning wheel. They found time to hoist rocks from fields, milk cows, and churn butter, all the while caring for sick neighbours, attending church, and taking part in community activities. Many of these resolute, stouthearted souls carried grain for miles to be ground into flour, fearful of encountering a bear, wolf, or some other wild animal along the way. Their stoicism, perseverance, and tenacity served them well. They were solid qualities that would be passed along and surface again in their daughters and granddaughters in the hockey rink.

Early in the century certain games received considerable attention in the newspapers. The press reports were often quite entertaining. Consider this *Toronto Star* reporter's description of the final period of a 1907 game between the Toronto Wellingtons and Waterloo:

Miss Dawson [of Waterloo] led the attacks and everybody except the goalkeeper — including the girl who fell down every time she made a rush — was there, and they gave the Torontonians the busiest five minutes you ever saw. If there hadn't been so many skirts in the way, Waterloo might have scored. But "them Wellintuns" just gathered around like a sewing circle listening to a piece of scandal, bent their knees until their skirts touched the ice, and — well, only a pair of shears or a 10.2 gun would have cleared the way to the nets.

Once Miss Dawson and Miss Allen [of Toronto] had a hot little argument over the disc and in the excitement they lost the puck. Even referee Ridpath could not locate it for some moments, but finally it was discovered in the shadow of the players' skirts.

The Waterloo ladies appeared in white sweaters and black skirts. They were bareheaded but some wore padded shoes. From beneath their goalkeeper's skirts, the ends of a pair of stout goalkeeper's pads projected. The Toronto girls were nattily clad in white sweaters with blue and white shoulders and collars with a "W" enclosed in a maple leaf on their breasts. All wore blue and white toques.

There was some floundering around in the opening minutes, and a few falls, prompting some rude fellows in the crowd to jeer. Then the girls lost their nervousness and settled down to play good hockey. The gypsum travelled from end to end but there was nothing doing. There were eager cries of "Come on, Dorothy, come on!" "Pass, Bessie, pass!" as the young women grew excited and wanted passes. Then Miss Hamilton accidentally smote a spectator with her stick and paused to beg his forgiveness.

A Sensation in Cornwall

In 1916 the Cornwall Vics introduced a teenage player named Albertine Lapansee who, for the next two seasons, dominated women's hockey as a scoring star. Albertine was sensational. She once scored 15 goals in a single game, and became such a drawing card that when the Vics agreed to play a game in Ottawa against the Alerts, manager Ernie Runions had to guarantee her appearance by a signed contract. Cornwall fans followed the Vics — and Albertine — much like a booster club would today. They filled the train that carried the Vics to Ottawa, and once there, they battled thousands of Ottawans for choice seats in Dey's Arena. Even on the coldest nights people came out to see Miss Lapansee, Cornwall's "Miracle Maid."

She was an outstanding stickhandler and shooter. One observer said she had a shot "as hard as Charlie Conacher's." Indeed, she scored five out of the six goals for Cornwall in her first clash with the Alerts, and "gave a whirlwind display of skating, checking, and scoring that was sufficient to make the average male pro blush with envy," said the Ottawa Citizen.

On February 6, 1917, Miss Lapansee scored all three goals in Cornwall's win over the Montreal Westerns. The crowd was reported to be the largest ever to witness a game between women, although no attendance figures were given. Scoring summaries of the era, while incomplete, indicate Miss Lapansee scored over 80 percent of her team's goals during the 1916–17 season.

A week later, in a game against the Montreal Westerns, Miss Lapansee and Miss Deloro of the Westerns came close to having a battle royal. Deloro checked the Cornwall girl tenaciously from the opening whistle and then bumped her hard into the fence during the second period. Miss Lapansee spun around, took off her gloves, and told her opponent to stop such tactics or "she would stop her once and for all." Miss Deloro moved forward and said, "I'm not afraid of you, even if you are from Cornwall. I'll be glad to meet you after the game and we'll settle this the way the men do."

There was no opportunity for punching or hair pulling after the contest because the victorious Cornwall team was in a great hurry to catch their train. During the same game, one lady threw her stick at a man who made uncomplimentary remarks about her, another player fainted, and part of the crowd threatened one of the goal umpires for giving what they thought was an unjust decision. "The war in Europe," wrote one reporter, "has nothing on these ladies' hockey games."

The next season Cornwall attracted even more publicity, largely thanks to Albertine Lapansee's scoring prowess, and the Vics sailed through an undefeated season. "Albertine," said proud manager Runions, "is playing 100 percent better than last season, and in the games against the [Montreal] Telegraphers she did really remarkable work. None of the stars in the National Hockey Association can teach this little lady anything about the fine points of the game."

After two spectacular seasons like that, one would assume Albertine scored all her team's goals in 1918–19. But when I tried to find out more about the Miracle Maid, I came up with nothing. Albertine Lapansee simply vanished! Finally, after a bit of detective work, I found a relative of Albertine's, a man named Connie Lapansee, who was able to solve the mystery. "In 1918," Connie told me, "Albertine went to New York City and had a sex change operation." The Miracle Maid had become a man, married, and eventually settled down and opened a gas station not far from Cornwall under the name of Albert Smyth.

The Wellingtons won by a score of 6–0. About 700 fans witnessed the match. Many came to laugh but stayed to admire.

FOR A BRIEF TIME during the mining boom in Northern Ontario (or New Ontario as it was then called), hockey was front-page news. Many of the best male players of the era performed for teams in Cobalt and Haileybury. Incredibly, in 1909, the two small towns were granted membership in the National Hockey Association, forerunner to the NHL. The miners

E. CLARK
L. WING

MRS. J. WEST
GOAL

L. MEYERS
R. WING

A. LAGREE
C. POINT

COBALT

A. TRIPP
ROVER

1910 1911

C. TRIPP
MASCOTT

TEMISKAMING LEAGUE

E. ROACH
C. POINT

P. TRIPP
CENTRE

LADIES HOCKEY TEAM

MC GREA'S
STUDIO

MRS. D. QUINN
POINT

wanted the best hockey money could buy, and players were paid enormous salaries to join NHA teams. Northern fans introduced a new method of celebrating a victory — by throwing money on the ice. One night there was so much money thrown that Big Billy Nicholson, Haileybury's enterprising 300-pound goaltender, scooped up the cash and piled it in front of his net. Then he grabbed a washtub, turned it upside down over the loot, and sat on the tub. It was an unexpected bonus to his already fat salary. Big Billy was the father of Helen Nicholson, who grew up to be one of the premier players in women's hockey in the 1930s.

Women's hockey during this brief era attracted almost as much attention as the NHA brand. The games between Cobalt and archrival Haileybury were bitterly contested, producing fireworks and fisticuffs. Let us examine the 1911 season and a four-game series between the clubs with the coveted O'Brien Trophy at stake. Excerpts are from the *Cobalt Daily Nugget* and most appeared on the front page:

Tonight's game [the second in the series] between the Cobalt and Haileybury girls' teams will be a hummer. The Haileybury people are coming down by the carload to cheer for their players. The local girls will not be lacking for support either, and if the rink is not packed to capacity all indications must not be believed. The attendance at the last game here [the first in the series] between the girls' teams (Haileybury 2, Cobalt 0) was the largest of the season, but it will be small in comparison to the crowd that will be on hand tonight.

The local girls have just received new suits — green and white sweaters, toques and stockings, and they are confident that they will trim the Haileybury girls to a standstill. Then, on the other hand, the girls from the north are equally as confident that they will take home the big end of the score, and they have not been wasting time when they should have been practicing. There will be three carloads of people down with the team, and it's up to the Cobalt people to wear the green and white and cheer for the home brews.

After a description of the opening minutes of play in the second game, the sportswriter for the *Cobalt Daily Nugget* recounted a most unusual situation: "Then an offside resulted in a face-off right in the Haileybury net, but after an exciting half minute the puck was banged out. . . ." Several more paragraphs vividly portrayed the action until play was halted just before halftime: "Miss Powers took a rest [was penalized] and just then the boards at one end of the rink broke out, precipitating several people on to the ice, but no one was hurt and after repairs the game was resumed. . . ." In the second half play became quite rough: "At this point the hard checking commenced. Miss Ferguson took two minutes rest and Miss Powers was knocked out in a collision with a Cobalt forward. . . ."

The game ended with both goaltenders, Miss McPharland of Haileybury and Mrs. West of Cobalt, getting credit for a shutout. Fifty years or more later, in the sixties, when I hired a baby-sitter for my expanding family in Toronto, an elderly sitter I knew as "Mac" McPharland told me she loved hockey and had been a goalie as a young woman living in Northern Ontario. It wasn't until I began researching this book that I made the connection. How I wish now I had taken time to ask her about her hockey career.

There was talk of the teams playing overtime following the scoreless contest, but the women were eager to attend an important function at the Cobalt Hotel and the idea was rejected. The function was a banquet for the male and female players of Haileybury and Cobalt. Players of both sexes desired the pleasure of one another's company while the evening was still comparatively young.

Art Throop, manager of the Haileybury team, and Billy Nicholson, the veteran goal-tender, expressed their pleasure at being present and thanked the Cobalt girls for their hospitality. Ada Tripp, captain of the Cobalt club, although one eye was closed and bandaged as the result of an accident during the game, said she was glad of the opportunity to meet the visitors socially as well as on the ice. Miss Tripp's little sister Carla, Cobalt's mascot, had been escorted around the arena prior to the game and had received a rousing ovation.

Those who witnessed the scoreless tie between Haileybury and Cobalt in the Cobalt rink were anxious to be on hand for the third game in the series for the O'Brien Trophy. The *Cobalt Daily Nugget* opined:

> Those who saw the game were well pleased with the class of hockey played, because hockey played by the girls has attained a standing in the estimation of the fans never before held. The game has passed the comedy stage and lovers of the sport take as much interest in the game played by the fair ones as they do when two men's teams are engaged in battle. The crowds at the girls' games are proof of this.

All the goodwill and friendly kibitzing between the teams at the Cobalt Hotel banquet disappeared when the women donned their skates for the game two nights later back in Haileybury. The *Nugget* headline on page one read: ANOTHER NO-SCORE GAME WAS PLAYED. HAILEYBURY AND COBALT GIRLS FIGURE IN SOMEWHAT STRENUOUS CONTEST.

Strenuous? It was more like a slugfest, a donnybrook. Here is a condensed edition of the *Nugget* sportswriter's report:

> Haileybury, March 4: The old expression used in rough senior hockey, that it is no "ladies" game, will have to be put on the shelf, and a new saying looked up after last night's scoreless game in Haileybury between the Cobalt and Haileybury maidens. The fair sex demonstrated to about 1000 fans that they could rough it up with the best of them.
>
> From the outset, it was apparent that certain players on each team were out for each other. In the second half, Miss Mahoney and Miss MacKay of the local team, mixed matters up with Miss Meyers of the visitors' lineup and all three were sent to the penalty bench. Then a few

minutes later, Referee Oke got into a mixup with some Cobalt supporters on the South side of the rink and there was a free-for-all fight on the ice between the spectators. Chief Miller and Constable Collins put an end to the affair and a couple of Cobalt men were placed under arrest.

Some Cobalt supporters, it is said, were calling the girls from Haileybury names that could scarcely be put in print. Instead of notifying the police, Referee Teddy Oke tried to stop the fracas. This made it worse and when Miss Mahoney bodied Miss Clarke, some spectators grabbed her and held her to the fence. Oke skated over, and raised his bell to strike the man, but before he could hit him, the fellow threw his skates at Teddy, cutting the bridge of his nose to the bone. The referee grabbed Miss Mahoney's stick, and started in to hit the fellow who hit him. This started the free-for-all that was put to an end by the two policemen. Altogether the whole affair is most regrettable, and will no doubt put an end to ladies' hockey in New Ontario.

Early in the game Miss Meyers of Cobalt was given a penalty — one minute for slashing — but she refused to go off, maintaining her innocence. The team captain finally persuaded her to take her punishment. When she returned to the ice, she found herself involved in a costly offside. The Cobalt attackers didn't hear the whistle and went in and scored, touching off quite a loud argument when referee Oke decided the goal wouldn't count. Moments later one of the rink lights "went bad." During the interval, the referee had to search for his bell. Fifteen minutes passed before he found it.

For the visitors, Miss Meyers, while inclined to be rough, played the best game on the ice, although Miss P. Tripp was easily a close second. Final score: Haileybury 0, Cobalt 0.

The fourth game in the series was played back in Cobalt two nights later. The final score was 2–2, and when the Cobalt women requested an overtime period to settle things, the visitors from Haileybury refused. This angered the hometown girls, who faced-off the puck, went in, and scored into the empty net, claiming victory by a score of 3–2.

Nobody involved in this series seemed to know under what conditions it was played. Haileybury officials said they believed total goals should decide the championship, while Cobalt said the games should be counted. On March 11 the trustees ruled that the Haileybury team would have their names engraved on the trophy, having outscored Cobalt 4 goals to 2 in the series. To no one's surprise, Cobalt's empty-net goal in the final match was disallowed.

So ended one of the most bitterly contested series in the early history of women's hockey. But the appeal of the game had been established. Women had proven they could play the game and inflame the fans. Much more was to come.

2

Taking the Game Seriously

CAN YOU IMAGINE your great grandmother playing hockey outdoors in bitterly cold weather, wearing a long skirt, a bulky sweater, and a stocking cap? In place of a stocking cap she might wear a tam — or possibly a toque with a long tassle that often fell over her eyes, blocking her vision and tickling her nose. Her long hair would be tucked under her cap and held in place with a number of combs. Early in this century one could see such sights whenever and wherever women played hockey.

But some women couldn't play. It simply wasn't allowed. As late as 1914, the Amateur Athletic Union of Canada wouldn't allow women to take part in the sports or activities they controlled. A small number of women were permitted to take part in Olympic events beginning in 1900 — but only in golf and tennis. It wasn't until 1912 that women swimmers appeared at the Stockholm Olympics, and the first athletic events for women were part of the 1928 Olympics in Amsterdam.

University women's team,
Burwash Hall, Victoria College
Playing Field, 1910.

(City of Toronto Archives)

There were no women joggers early in the century. During that era, newspapers like the Toronto *Globe*, reflecting the opinion of the masses, decided that the simple act of running was terribly unladylike:

> She can swim, she can dance, she can ride: all these things she can do admirably and with ease to herself. But to run, nature most surely did not construct her. She can do it after a fashion, just as the domestic hen will on occasion make shift to fly; but the movement is unconstrained and awkward — may we say without disrespect? — a kind of precipitate waddle with neither grace, fitness or dignity.

I shudder to think of how the writer would view a woman barrelling up the ice, elbows flying, hands swinging a hockey stick.

Some women were cautioned by their family doctors to avoid taking part in any physical activity aside from household chores. The medical profession, which was predominantly male, took note of women's escalating participation in sports and began issuing stern warnings against a number of physical pursuits, such as cycling, running, and games that could lead to body contact — like hockey. Vigorous activity on the playing fields, women were cautioned, could lead to a disturbance of the menstrual cycle and result in considerable damage to the reproductive organs.

Doctors weren't the only professional men handing out advice that made women think twice before picking up a hockey stick or a tennis racquet. Educators, clergymen, university athletic directors, and others concerned with female behaviour and morality admonished young women who became enamoured of competitive sports. "Remember, young ladies," they were warned, "participation in sports may foster manly qualities, like boldness, initiative, pride and a spirit of independence." That was enough to frighten many young damsels into a state of near-paralysis. Others rather fancied such qualities.

Opponents of women cyclists claimed that the shape of the bicycle seat would stimulate the rider sexually, that sweating from cycling would lead to body odour and even disease. One lady cyclist, Louise Bresbois of Montreal, was treated rudely by a fan in 1882 when she competed in a professional race on her penny farthing bicycle. Riding in her home city, she was yanked from her bicycle by an angry young man as she zoomed by at full speed.

But the joy of participation was strong, and many women risked censure by taking part in sports like tennis, golf, and hockey. In 1900 a ladies' hockey team from Brandon, Manitoba, actually defeated a men's team representing a local bank.

Accustomed to being attacked by men who pegged them as homebodies and nothing more, sports-minded women ignored the gibes they received for hitching up a skirt and racing around the bases or dribbling a basketball down the court. But jeers turned to cheers when Percy Page, a teacher at McDougall Commercial High School in Edmonton, recruited some students and graduates of the school and formed the Edmonton Grads, the greatest women's basketball team ever assembled. Obviously Percy was cut from a unique mould, unlike most males of the era. From 1915 to 1940 the Grads compiled a record of 502 wins and only 20 defeats.

But even the talented Grads left some columnists unimpressed. Noted Vancouver *Sun* sportswriter Andy Lytle expressed his contempt:

> Many of these women athletes are leather-limbed and inclined to flat chests. I say you can't have bodily contact without danger to the soft bodies of women. In Vancouver the girls play lacrosse and they are constantly going to the doctor for treatment. They cannot pad their bodies to prevent injury. It's a rough game and it takes the polish off girls.

Women athletes, sans polish, tried to ignore the old fogies who attacked them and kept right on playing.

By the end of World War I, hockey players were beginning to discard those bulky skirts ("I couldn't even see my feet when I started up the ice," one of them complained) in favour of knee-length bloomers. Helen Gurley, who played on the University of Toronto team in that era, says: "The bloomers came in at the end of the war. In the early twenties they were shortened to just above the knee. By the late twenties we started to wear a hockey pant that was similar to the pant they wear today except that they were narrower and not as well-padded. In my day some of the girls wore small shin pads or even magazines under their long stockings."

This was an era when Canadian women blossomed in several sports. The war that took thousands of young lives changed Canadian attitudes. Barriers that had held women back from many pursuits for decades were quietly being overturned. Not only were women seizing opportunities that had once been denied them, they were fulfilling a need to forget the wartime horrors by indulging in carefree pastimes and games of fun. Skating was one of them, hockey another.

Skating, tobogganing, snowshoeing, skiing — Canadian women have always been willing participants in all of the popular winter sports. At one time Montreal women enjoyed the thrills of the long toboggan slides located on Côte St-Antoine near Sherbrooke Street. One was a natural slide covering 2,400 feet. The other two were artificial, each 1,500 feet long.

Of all the winter sports, women enjoyed skating the most. But early on they had to deal with some annoying social restrictions before taking part. In the mid-1800s women rarely experienced the pleasure of fun on blades. Skating for young females was all but forbidden by straitlaced parents. It was fine for sons to strap on blades and fly over the river's thick ice, but their sisters stayed home. How such an innocent pastime could be considered unladylike or the least bit damaging to one's reputation is difficult to understand, but halfway through the last century that was the case. Well-bred young women didn't skate.

Fortunately it wasn't long before a handful of pioneer women poohpoohed that fatuous notion and became trailblazers, taking up the sport despite the objections of their elders. In no time at all thousands followed suit. Soon skating parties became highly popular winter events. They were, after all, ideal occasions for girls to meet boys. Although no survey has ever been taken, it would be interesting to know what percentage of married Canadians first met their mate-to-be on a skating rink.

By 1917 the long skirts were gone and players like Eva Ault of Ottawa were playing in less constrictive bloomers.

(National Archives of Canada)

In *Montreal: Island City of the St. Lawrence,* Kathleen Jenkins praises one place where skaters assembled in great numbers — the Victoria Rink, site of the first Stanley Cup playoff game:

Of all the skating establishments in Montreal, none could surpass the Victoria Rink on Drummond Street. Opened in 1862, its exclusive nature was reflected in the use of the word "club" — an elastic term, perhaps, since in 1882, it boasted of two thousand members. The archlike roof rose to a height of 52 feet above the great stretch of ice, 200 feet by 80 feet in size. Around the walls, a ten-foot platform provided ample space for onlookers, while a music gallery met the needs of the band. Windows on three sides admitted plenty of daylight, and at night five hundred gas jets gave a brilliant illumination. The Victoria was adjudged the largest and best rink in either Europe or North America.

Historian Jenkins credits women for the gradual move toward indoor ice in the 1800s:

It seems likely that the feminine influence was partly responsible for the trend to indoor rinks. For although the natural ice of the St. Lawrence had met the needs of the less sophisticated times, its users were exposed to the full blast of the winter winds and the snow. Thus while ordinary folk still flocked to the improvised skating areas on the river, the canal and the vacant lots, society moved under cover.

The 18th-century woman, having shaken off the same chains that had bound her parents, finally was able to experience the joys of skating. And most became quite proficient on their blades. At the Victoria Rink soldiers from the British garrison often rented skates and tried to emulate the graceful moves of the Canadians. If they floundered and fell, there was a bonus. Several young women would glide over and hoist the red-faced soldier to his feet. Inevitably

women who skated were handed a bent stick by their brothers or boyfriends and shown how to push a puck or a ball around the ice.

What they wore was designed to keep them warm, not to protect them from bumps and bruises. Back then women didn't need protective equipment. But in the twenties and thirties, when leagues were formed and there were titles to be won, the game became more competitive and there was a perception that only the roughest, toughest girls played it. Many who didn't relish the harsh body contact and the frequent spills gave up the sport, often at the urging of their boyfriends or husbands. When a player emerged from a pileup nursing a bloody nose or a blackened eye, the man in her life was apt to plead with her to compete in tennis, golf, or even tiddlywinks — anything but hockey.

Thora Mills, a University of Toronto player in the twenties, reminiscing for a *Toronto Star* reporter in 1985, recalled the sparse equipment worn by members of her championship team in 1924–25:

Skating at Rideau Hall in Ottawa
in 1915. Note the sideboards and
end screens for hockey games.

(National Archives of Canada)

University of Toronto goalie. What each player wore was designed for maximum warmth.

(University of Toronto Archives)

We had arm and leg pads and, as the goalie on the team, I wore a chest protector. That was about it. We had no dressing rooms, no showers, no face masks and no indoor ice. We played outdoors almost all the time.

And we were very modest, undressing in front of each other very discreetly. We never stood up naked in front of the team. And we always travelled with a chaperone.

Mills recalled that the team manager of one of her college teams was Maryon Moody of Winnipeg, who later became the wife of Prime Minister Lester B. Pearson.

Varsity's tradition of excellence on ice stemmed from a challenge hurled at the skates of the Toronto women in 1921. McGill University suggested a match be played at a mutually convenient time. Varsity offered to host a game in the old Mutual Street Arena on February 24, 1922. It coincided nicely with a women's basketball tournament scheduled for the same week. Regular competition between Toronto, McGill, and Queen's took place until 1924–25 when McGill withdrew. Queen's stepped away from women's hockey in 1934–35 and only occasional games were played after that.

The university women of that era were the equal of any of the independent teams. In 1924–25 Varsity played in the Toronto Ladies Hockey League and not only won the championship but all playoff games, defeating Grimsby and the Ottawa Alerts to capture the Ladies' Ontario Hockey Association (LOHA) title. This was Thora Mills's team, and it is recognized as one of the most skillful ever to represent the University of Toronto. Star player Marian Hilliard was a charter inductee of the university's Sports Hall of Fame in 1987.

The university women withdrew from the Toronto hockey league after one season. "Demands on study time" was the reason given, but a bigger reason might have been the exceptionally rough play the women students encountered during their championship season.

Over the years many women played hockey wearing white figure skates — a Christmas gift from parents who envisioned their little darling doing leaps and twirls on the ice à la Sonja Henie. And when their Myrtle or Maud grabbed a hockey stick and joined her brothers in a game of shinny, the white skates seemed oddly out of place. The picks in the front of the blade tripped her up, and she was forced to skate with mincing little strides in order to stay upright. The smart girls either switched to regular hockey skates or they persuaded their fathers, once they recovered from the shock of seeing their daughters playing shinny, to grind off the picks.

Three university women try out their sticks at the University of Toronto's Varsity Stadium, 1910.
(City of Toronto Archives)

Women have been playing hockey at the University of Toronto — on and off — since 1900. For many of those seasons it was on an intramural basis only since travel costs prohibited competition with other universities. Until 1926, when Varsity Arena was constructed, the women played on an outdoor rink or at Aura Lee Park. Occasionally they gained entrance to Mutual Street Arena, home of the professional Toronto Maple Leafs.

The first star player on the Varsity roster was Marian Hilliard — later Dr. Marian Hilliard. She played university hockey for seven seasons — four in her arts and science course and three more in medicine. Helen Gurley recalls the time Marian Hilliard outplayed the multitalented Bobbie Rosenfeld in a game between the university girls and a City of Toronto team. Phyllis Griffiths was another prominent player of the day. Griffiths went on to join the *Toronto Star* as a columnist covering women's sports, which she did quite capably.

One of the star performers at Queen's was a young woman named Charlotte Whitton. In later life she became the mayor of Ottawa, and despite her own athletic background, fought vigorously to deny the fans in the capital of Sunday sport. She was a canny, controversial politician. Fred "Cyclone" Taylor, an early-day hockey superstar, recalls that Miss Whitton, then 12 years old, was at the game in Renfrew on the night he allegedly scored a goal against Ottawa while skating backward.

"Charlotte was more than an excellent hockey player," Gurley has stated. "Back at Renfrew Collegiate she was quite a versatile track star. Won just about everything every year."

Helen Gurley, in researching her book *A Century to Remember*, a history of women's sport at the University of Toronto, found it difficult to pinpoint where and when games outside the realm of college games were played. "These games weren't well publicized because the girls weren't interested in a lot of fanfare. They simply organized teams and played exhibition games. It was a case of 'Let's our team play yours' and away they'd go."

Gurley credits the persistence of Marie Parks for boosting women's hockey through these difficult years: "She was the backbone of intercollegiate hockey at that time. At the university she was the secretary treasurer of the women's student council and she was the secretary treasurer of the women's athletic association — a real go-getter for close to 40 years. She was

instrumental in the founding of the Ladies' Ontario Hockey Association, and several hockey awards have been named in her honour. Women's hockey owes her a great deal."

By 1922 Varsity, McGill, and Queen's, having raised some funds for travel, were competing in the new Women's Collegiate Ice Hockey League for the Beattie Ramsay Trophy, named after one of the star male players on Canada's Olympic hockey team.

EARLY-DAY RECORDS SHOW that men were playing hockey in Alberta in the 1890s, with women following suit a year or two later. The *Medicine Hat Times* reports that a game between ladies wearing dresses was played on March 11, 1897. The *Times* wasn't able to provide any details on the match because spectators were barred from the proceedings. By 1899 women were playing hockey in Edmonton.

Early in the century Banff, Alberta, was the site of many women's games. They were played on an outdoor rink, and for many years they were scheduled in conjunction with the annual Banff Winter Carnival. In 1908 a sizable crowd turned out to watch a team of Banff women shut out the Calgary Barracks Club 2–0. The Rocky Mountain Park Trophy was presented to the winners.

In the twenties a number of teams, including several representing various churches, competed against one another in Calgary. The Calgary Hollies (not a church team) became the most prominent. In 1927 the Hollies captured the Banff tournament and went on to blank the Edmonton Monarchs 1–0 in overtime to add the Alberta ladies' title to their laurels. The Monarchs came looking for revenge the following season and edged the Hollies 1–0 to bring the title north to Edmonton.

At about the same time the Western Inter-Varsity Athletic Union was formed, with the University of Saskatchewan icing the first women's team. Genevra "Ginger" Catherwood, sister to the renowned Olympic high jumper Ethel Catherwood, was the star player on the team.

Former teammate Ellen Andreason told historian Joe Zeman: "When Genevra came down the ice, everyone stayed out of her way." On a two-game road trip to Manitoba in 1921 "Ginger" Catherwood scored eight of her team's goals in a 9–1 rout of Winnipeg, and an astonishing 12 goals in a follow-up humiliation of the Brandon team.

The Ottawa Alerts, champions of eastern Canada. Star player Shirley Moulds is directly behind the trophy, centre row.

(National Archives of Canada)

Ginger and Ethel Catherwood were two of the best women athletes in Canada in the twenties. When they came to Toronto, they were taken under the wing of multimillionaire Teddy Oke. He sent them to business school and then placed them in his brokerage office, which was staffed with a number of outstanding women athletes. Ethel, whose beauty attracted photographers in droves, developed into the world's best high jumper and won a gold medal for Canada with a leap of five feet, two point seven inches at the 1928 Olympics in Amsterdam. A year later the Catherwood sisters moved to the United States.

IN MARCH 1922 the famous Ottawa Alerts, champions of eastern Canada, met the North Toronto Ladies team in a home-and-home series. In Ottawa the teams played to a scoreless tie. According to the *Toronto Star* 4,000 fans saw the game and "waxed very enthusiastic over the superb hockey displayed." The *Star* billed the return match, a 1–0 North Toronto victory, as one of the best exhibitions of ladies' hockey ever staged:

> Ottawa has a real star in Miss Eva Ault, their centre player, who is credited with scoring at least one goal in practically every game she has played.

> Several players "took the count" from heavy checks and Miss Marion Giles, a little tot on the Ottawa team, received a gash over the eye when Miss Mitchell, a North Toronto defense player, bumped her as she shot on goal. The smallest member of the Ottawa team, Miss Shirley Moulds, a 15-year-old youngster with her hair down her back, was the best player on the ice but she couldn't stand up under the heavy bodying of the Toronto girls.

The *Star* added the following editorial comment:

> If ladies hockey is to be made a success, body checking must be eliminated. That is too rough a method of checking for women to employ. Games must be handled by strict referees and

penalties handed out for every move that is not according to the Hoyle of hockey. Tripping, charging, shoving and holding should not be tolerated for a moment. The fans like to see the ladies perform, but they do not want to see any roughness creep into the contests.

In March 1923 the Alerts bounced back to win the Ontario ladies' title after a two-game series with North Toronto. Ottawa won by scores of 1–0 on home ice and 5–2 in Toronto. The outstanding player in the series was North Toronto's Bobbie Rosenfeld. She was the fastest player on the ice and possessed an awesome ability to stickhandle. Her teammates were content to let her do most of the work, which is why they lost. One reporter wrote:

> When Miss Rosenfeld grabbed the puck none of her teammates had the brains to start down to the other goal and be ready to help her out by taking a pass or slamming in a rebound. Miss Moulds of Ottawa has almost as much speed as Miss Rosenfeld but she lacked the Toronto girl's stamina. She took her bumps gamely and broke away to score four of her team's goals.

> There was a little flare-up at the end. One Ottawa girl wanted to scratch Miss Preston because of her alleged rough play.

On December 8, 1924, Miss Janet Allan, formerly of Stratford and later a Toronto resident, was elected president of the Ladies' Ontario Hockey Association. First vice president was Miss E. E. Ault of Ottawa; second vice president, W. H. Legg of London; secretary treasurer, Miss B. Rosenfeld of Toronto; executive, Miss Nichols of Galt, Miss Anderson of Ottawa, Miss Semple of Whitby, and Miss Webb of Galt. Dr. Robertson of Stratford was unable to attend the meeting, but the trophy donated by him was presented to the Ottawa Alerts by William Eason, president of the Ontario Hockey Association.

It was decided that for the 1925 season only officials of those clubs that had paid their annual fees prior to the annual meeting would be allowed to vote. It was further decided that the schedule would begin earlier and that a fund would be established to enable clubs to decide a Canadian championship.

The incomparable Marian Hilliard in her heyday in the 1920s.
(University of Toronto Archives)

A motion was passed that only bona fide residents be allowed to compete in the LOHA series, and there was discussion about organizing an intermediate series. Another long discussion ensued over allowing men to hold office in the LOHA. President Allan favoured their inclusion and that opinion prevailed.

In the mid-1920s the name Preston began surfacing in reports of women's hockey. It was the beginning of what would later become one of the greatest dynasties in the history of female hockey. In March 1924 a Preston team journeyed to London, Ontario, and shut out that city's AAA team 2–0. London's Lucy Milne shed a few tears after the game. She inadvertently shot the puck into her own net during the 20-minute overtime period, which proved to be the winning goal for the visitors.

But Preston wasn't quite ready to make a major impact on women's hockey. Later that month a speedy North Toronto women's team defeated them 2–1 in the LOHA finals. Bobbie Rosenfeld, described as "the superwoman of ladies' hockey" by Preston reporters, scored the winning goal in the third period.

Meanwhile the University of Toronto team was bowling over all competition. The Varsity girls defeated Grimsby 3–0 and 2–0 in a series and later captured the City of Toronto title.

On March 14, 1924, the collegians walloped the highly regarded Ottawa Alerts 5–1 in the first game of a home-and-home series for "the championship of Ontario." The first game in Ottawa attracted a good-size crowd, and the Varsity girls displayed excellent speed, backchecking ability, and combination play. Olive Mews and Marian Hilliard were the best players on the ice for Varsity, and Shirley Moulds was a constant threat for the Alerts. Referee Bill Smith didn't call a single penalty.

A week later, back in Toronto, Varsity and Ottawa fought to a 1–1 tie. Marian Hilliard amazed the onlookers with her speed and clever playmaking, while Shirley Moulds and Marion Giles of Ottawa unleashed some of the hardest shots ever seen in women's hockey.

Varsity goalie Thora McIlroy finished the season with a remarkable record, allowing only six goals against all competition. Doris Ross was the leading scorer on the team, and Marian Hilliard was the top playmaker, setting up most of the goals scored by her teammates. Hilliard was recognized as the best all-round athlete at the university. Olive Mews and Marjorie Fenwick claimed they learned their hockey from playing "shinny on the pond" in their home province of Newfoundland.

The referee for the final match was hockey idol Harry Watson, another native of Newfoundland and the greatest amateur player in the world. Watson was the top Canadian player on Canada's 1924 championship Olympic team and scored 13 of 30 goals in a single game against Czechoslovakia.

Two years later the Toronto Patterson Pats won the championship of the Toronto Hockey League by defeating Aura Lee in a two-game playoff series. The Pats won the opener 3–0; the second game was a scoreless tie. Advancing against London, winners of the western section over Stratford and Galt, the Pats competed for further honours in the LOHA. They recorded consecutive shutouts against London, winning 3–0 and 2–0, and advanced to the eastern finals against the Ottawa Rowing Club.

Bobbie Rosenfeld scored all her team's goals in leading the Pats to a 4–0 shutout in the opener, and goalie Annie Miller was sensational in the Toronto net. Showing great courage

time and again, she would dive into a group of milling players and trap the rubber in her glove. Back in Ottawa a week later, Rosenfeld was again unstoppable and scored both Toronto goals in a 2–0 victory. She had the unique distinction of scoring all the goals in the two-game series, while goalie Miller stopped Ottawa scoring threat Shirley Moulds at least a dozen times.

The Patterson Pats were back on top of the Toronto Hockey League again in 1927. By defeating Aura Lee 4–1 and 1–0 at the Ravina Rink on March 4, the Pats captured the series 5–1 and earned the right to advance against the winner of a London–Forest series in the provincial playoffs.

Goaltending was once more a strong point for the Pats. Annie Miller allowed only two goals in the entire season's play. The attack was led by Bobbie Rosenfeld and Winnie Simpson, while Janet Allan and Doris Ross anchored the defence.

The following day Janet Allan was reelected president of the Ladies' Ontario Hockey Association at the annual meeting. Represented were the Ottawa Rowing Club, Ottawa Alerts, Forest, London, and the Toronto Hockey League. It was decided that London and Forest had to declare a winner by March 12. The winning team from that series would advance against the Toronto Pats on or before March 19. By that time the Ottawa Rowing Club and the Ottawa Alerts promised to have a champion declared and the finals would take place March 26.

On March 13 Forest edged London 1–0 in a thrilling one-game playoff and qualified to meet the Pats in a home-and-home series. On March 20 the Pats blanked Forest 2–0 at London. Both teams drew a large number of supporters to the arena in Toronto for game two. The Forest girls, young and inexperienced, were lost on the large ice surface, and the Pats had no difficulty in shutting them out again, this time by 7–0. The Pats won the round 9–0, and the victory led to a full headline across the top of the *Toronto Star* sports page the following day.

Bobbie Rosenfeld scored three of the Pats' goals, Dot Roffey had two, and singles went to Winnie Simpson and Casey McLean. The *Toronto Star* reporter at the game was critical of the visitors' goaltending and quite impressed with the skills of Rosenfeld and McLean:

Miss Allpaugh in the Forest goal was weak on shots that travelled through the air. She guarded her nets mostly in a floor scrubbing position and, being a small girl, left most of the upper part of her nets unprotected.

In Bobbie Rosenfeld and Casey McLean, the Pats have two players who could earn a place on any O.H.A. (men's) junior team. Both are speedy and good stickhandlers and pack a shot that has plenty of steam on it. Miss McLean scored a goal with a shot that blazed in shoulder high and hit the top of the net over the head of the Forest goalkeeper. Miss Rosenfeld was the best player on the ice but she spoiled her effectiveness around the net by failing to pass the puck.

The referee for the Toronto game was the renowned Fred Waghorne, who was a referee for 50 years and was the first man to drop the puck for face-offs instead of placing it between the sticks of opposing centres and shouting, "Play!" He also introduced the referee's whistle to hockey, replacing the hand bell that had been used for many years.

The powerful Pats received a rude surprise when they met the Ottawa Rowing Club (winners over the Alerts) in the provincial finals. Playing on home ice, the Rowing Club stunned the Pats 3–0 in the first game of the home-and-home series. It was the Pats' first loss in two seasons of play. Shirley Moulds scored goals one and three for Ottawa, and Ruby Gooding received credit for the second after McLean accidentally knocked the puck into her own net.

Back in Toronto on April 5 the Pats scored a 2–0 shutout over the Rowing Club, with Bobbie Rosenfeld and Casey McLean scoring the goals. But the green-clad Pats fell one goal short and the Rowing Club girls, in their red-and-blue uniforms, claimed the Ontario championship.

Another Toronto team was more fortunate that season. The University of Toronto women's team defeated Queen's 2–1 and 2–0 to capture the intercollegiate championship. Toronto's Marian Hilliard was the best player on the ice and received wave after wave of applause for her work.

The Toronto Pats won the 1929 LOHA title, defeating the Solloway-Mills ladies from Ottawa 1–0 in game one on Toronto ice. Back in Ottawa the teams skated to a 2–2 tie. Bobbie Rosenfeld's tying goal in game two was the deciding marker in the series. Goalie Annie Miller sparkled throughout the short series.

The day after the Pats became champions Alexandrine Gibb wrote:

The Ottawa lassies who crossed sticks with Patterson's Pats in the hockey finals looked more like a school girls' team than anything belonging to a brokerage firm. They must have picked all the beauties from in and around Ottawa and taught them how to play hockey. From the tiny Olive Barr in goal, with her fair hair and innocent, child-like face to the tallest defence girl, they were all easy to look at.

Ottawa Solloway-Mills, Ottawa and District champions, 1928-29.
(Author's Collection)

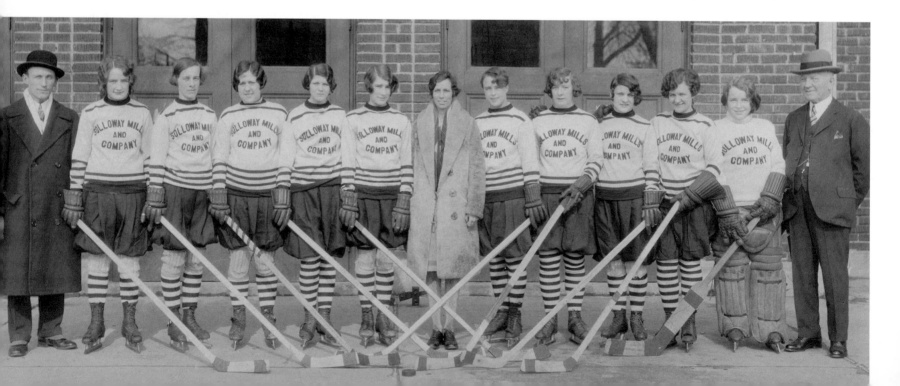

Any referee who would accept a fee to handle one of their games would be hard-boiled. Their average age was 18 — and any one of them could go to the Atlantic City parade.

"Dynamite" was the nickname tacked on to Vida Gowland. A big girl, she had a strong stride and plenty of speed. So much speed that sometimes it was impossible to stop and she rammed the boards so hard at the end of her journey she jarred the fence.

All that the girls got who visited the penalty bench was a lift up and down. There was no gate entrance so the naughty girls were forced to get assistance over the high boards.

The Pats then journeyed to Montreal where they appeared at the big winter carnival and played against the Quebec champions. Gibb reported:

The Pats did their bit toward helping Montreal sporting organizations in the program for charity by paying their own expenses here to win a mythical Canadian championship by a 2–0 score from the Quebec champions, the Northern Electric Verdun team.

If the Pats play as good hockey against Ottawa today for the Ontario title as they did in their thirty minutes of play last night in Montreal, the Toronto team will win the real title of Ontario champions.

The Montreal team was clad in maroon sweaters and short maroon skirts. Over 12,000 people were at the Forum. Nellie Jones of Montreal won the special hockey race for girls from Alice Hackett of Toronto.

The following day the Toronto girls and Ottawa fought to a 2–2 tie in a game that featured plenty of rough play and some stick swinging. The referee appeared to enjoy watching the girls exchange body slams and cracks across the ankles, and his work was severely criticized by Gibb in the *Toronto Star:*

The time has come when the L.O.H.A. executive had better step in and inform the male hockey officials who get paid for officiating at the ladies' hockey games that it isn't a joke. In an Ontario final with all the tussle and anxiety to win, there is bound to be reason for calling some penalties. But there weren't any called in the Ottawa hockey final for girls at Ottawa Saturday afternoon — and there should have been plenty for illegal body checking and slashing. That will kill the game quicker than anything else.

Why a man who is paid for a job thinks it is a joke and does not take it seriously is beyond me, but just because it is girls' hockey some of these men do not take it as anything but a big holiday. It would not be such fun if they did not get paid for it. Strange to say it is the men who come along and offer their services gratis who realize that the game means serious business to the girls. Of course, men of this calibre are the best referees in the game. They know how important these games are to the girls and that it means as much to the feminine portion of sport as the big NHL games do in the men's series.

A year later the eagerly anticipated rematch between Toronto and Ottawa was cancelled when the Ottawa girls were disqualified for failing to send in players' certificates within the required time. The decision to disqualify the Alerts practically killed any interest in the senior women's finals for 1930.

Queen's Goalie Introduces Face Mask

In 1927 a female goalie from Queen's made history by becoming the first player to wear a goalie face mask. Stewart Bell, writing in the Vancouver Sun in 1992, noted that his grandmother, Elizabeth Graham, decided to wear a wire fencing mask to protect her face during intercollegiate games. Her appearance in goal wearing the protective device rated one small paragraph in the Montreal Star: "The Queen's goalie gave the fans a surprise when she stepped into the nets and then donned a fencing mask. It was safety first with her and even at that she can't be blamed for her precautionary methods."

Three years later, in 1930, NHL goalie Clint Benedict wore a crude leather face mask to protect a broken nose, but he tossed the face guard away after one or two games. It wasn't until November 1, 1959, that Montreal's Jacques Plante began wearing a mask in every game he played. But he followed Elizabeth Graham's commonsense lead by more than three decades.

Elva McKay, the 15-year-old goaltender from Chalk River, Ontario.

(Author's Collection)

The LOHA declared that Chalk River would replace the Alerts in the provincial finals. It was agreed that the teams would meet at the Montreal Forum in a sudden-death game during the annual carnival. A large crowd turned out to see the Pats humiliate the inexperienced Chalk River girls 4–0. Chalk River's 15-year-old goaltender Elva McKay was bombarded with shots, and whenever Chalk River invaded the Pats' end of the rink, they were bounced to the ice by Vida Gowland, who was nicknamed "Battleship" by the crowd for the manner in which she destroyed every puck carrier who came within reach.

Several members of the Montreal Canadiens and the Boston Bruins attended the afternoon game at the Forum and then prepared for their Stanley Cup game on the same ice that night. The Forum management was so pleased with the display put on by the girls that all gate receipts were turned over to them and complimentary tickets were issued for the Stanley Cup game.

Some American promoters on hand issued an invitation to the Pats to play an exhibition game in Atlantic City later in the year, but there is no record of that game ever having been played. However, the Pats' time in the limelight would soon be over. The women stickhandlers in Preston were polishing their game to perfection, and they were about to embark on a fabulous winning streak.

As the 1920s drew to a close, Toronto *Telegram* columnist Phyllis Griffiths looked with optimism to the future. During the 1929 season, she wrote:

As yet there is no women's hockey association governing the whole of Canada, but the women's leagues are beginning to get together and are arranging playdowns. The Montreal Association and the Verdun City and District Ladies Hockey League are anxious to play the L.O.H.A. winners (Aura Lee or Pats). Port Arthur and Fort William are playing off for the championship of the Thunder Bay Ladies League and up there the public is sold on feminine hockey. Last year there was an immense crowd at the game, in which Aura Lee defeated Port Arthur for the unofficial Dominion title. The University of Manitoba team, which is apparently at the top of the heap out in that province, is willing to come down to the head of the Lakes and meet the Thunder Bay champions in a playoff. In the event of winning, the Manitoba co-eds would agree to come still further east to meet the winners of the L.O.H.A.–Montreal play-off series. However, in view of the popularity of the games in the Thunder Bay district, the eastern champs will probably go up there to settle the championship.

Phyllis Griffiths ended her column with a scandalous story of two males who were nabbed trying to invade the dressing room of a women's team:

Remember the recent dispatch stating that two well-known men athletes tried to break into the dressing room of the St. Thomas girls' hockey team after a game in the town of Forest. Apologies from the offenders, who are both prominent rugby players, and who were apparently somewhat inebriated at the time, have closed the incident.

The female hockey player of the decade was Toronto's all-round athlete Bobbie Rosenfeld, a member of the 1928 Canadian Olympic track-and-field team and a gold medal winner.

Rosenfeld, whose first love was hockey, excelled at all sports except swimming. She joined Ethel Smith, Jane Bell, and Myrtle Cook and swept to Olympic gold in the 400-metre relay in world-record time.

Cook and Rosenfeld were champions in a number of sports and later both became respected sports journalists. When Canadian women began making inroads athletically in the 1920s, newspapers in major centres began hiring ex-athletes as reporters. As a result, there was more coverage of women's events in the twenties and thirties than there was in the four decades that followed. Even so, 87 percent of sports stories of the era were about male athletes and their events. In *Canada's Sporting Heroes*, S. F. Wise and Douglas Fisher called it "a striking anomaly, particularly in view of the fact that, ever since the dramatic display of the women's track team at the Amsterdam Olympics in 1928, Canadian women have always done better than men in international competition."

By 1929 Bobbie Rosenfeld was crippled with arthritis and spent eight months in bed and another year on crutches. Miraculously she was able to come back two years later to become the leading slugger in her women's softball league, and the following winter she was the top hockey player in Ontario. When arthritis flared up a second time in 1933, she retired from competitive sports and joined the Toronto *Globe and Mail*. Fellow columnist Robert Fulford once wrote of her:

> Bobbie was the first lesbian I knew as such, and every day her moment of greatest happiness — happiness I could see her almost physically trying to hide, for reasons it took me years to understand — coincided with her companion's arrival at our office to pick her up after work. One day this lady mentioned that she and Bobbie were looking for a new apartment and needed two bedrooms — one for Bobbie's trophies.

In 1949 Bobbie Rosenfeld was named Canadian Woman Athlete of the Half Century.

Bobbie (Fanny) Rosenfeld was the female player of the 1920s. She excelled at most sports and was an Olympic gold medallist.

(Canada's Sports Hall of Fame)

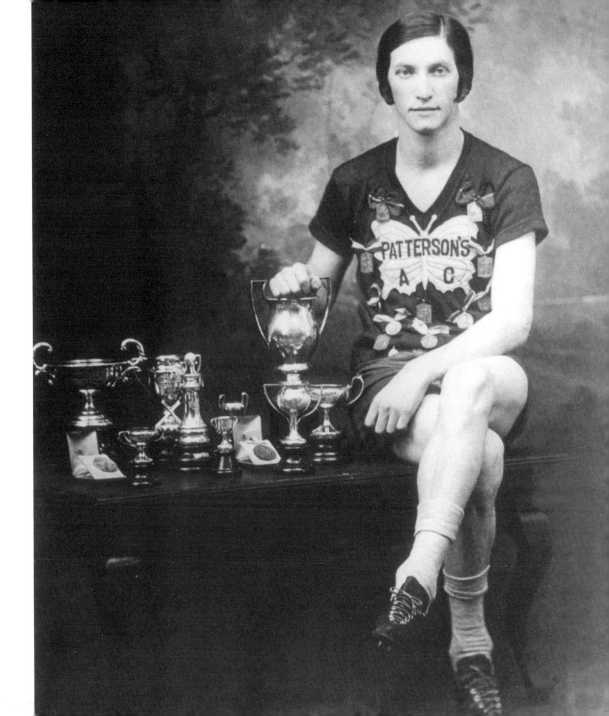

3

Roar of the Rivulettes

THE THIRTIES

BY THE THIRTIES Canadian women were everywhere in sport. Leila Brooks Potter, a well-known Canadian speed skater, closed out the 1920s by journeying to Detroit and winning both the quarter-mile and half-mile events in a major competition. An hour later she clipped five seconds off the previously recognized world record for the mile event.

The internationally famous Edmonton Grads basketball team sailed for Europe to test their skills against the best the Old World could produce. After playing nine games in several countries, they were undefeated and had outscored their opponents 664 points to 100. An undisputed world championship had been obtained for Canada.

Women polo players in Calgary not only formed three teams, but they and their ponies travelled 3,000 miles to represent their city and province in an international contest at the Westchester Biltmore Country Club outside New York City. And in September 1929 Halifax staged a marathon swimming championship for men and women. Sixteen men and 18 women

The renowned Preston Rivulettes. They dominated women's hockey throughout the 1930s.

(Hockey Hall of Fame)

took part, and the results were startling. The first 11 prizes were won by women. Writing in *Maclean's*, H. H. Roxborough said:

> Canadian women are not just knocking at the door of the world of sport, they have crashed the gate, swarmed the field and, in some games, driven mere man to the sidelines. Today, in Edmonton alone, a thousand girls are shooting basketballs into the cotton nets. A couple of years ago, nearly four hundred feminists were playing organized hockey, and some players have so progressed that one Toronto league has graduated from the free rinks and is operating before paying guests in an artificial-iced arena.

> A friend of mine, who, during the last season, coached a champion women's softball team, believes that girls are possibly better sports than men. In his judgment, the girls fight just as hard during a game and, when they win, the congratulations of friends do not result in uncontrollable pride. When they lose, they don't worry so much over defeat or think up so many alibis as men.

Concerned about the effects of strenuous games on the minds and bodies of young women, Roxborough sought an opinion from one of the most versatile and best informed athletes in Canada — Bobbie Rosenfeld. She replied: "The extent to which women can compete in athletics depends largely upon training. Any girl who satisfactorily passes a medical examination and who accepts and practises correct methods of training is capable of running eight hundred metres or continuing any other usual athletic pursuit." Roxborough concluded: "It thus seems evident that girl athletes, club managers, and women executive leaders are generally confident that no ill effects will follow the present strenuous participation of girls in sport."

Some of Roxborough's colleagues disagreed. One of them, Andy Lytle, penned an article called "Girls Shouldn't Do It!" for *Chatelaine* in 1933. Among other things he wrote:

There are sports, I hold, for which women are physically and temperamentally unfitted, and among these I would place all those which exact too much exertion to perform expeditiously and skillfully, as well as those which bring the inevitable concomitants of fatigue and exhaustion in their wake.

Ice hockey is a game, fortunately indulged in by comparatively few girls teams, even as in lacrosse, for which the soft, yielding flesh with which Nature equips the sex, makes them wholly unsuited, to say nothing of the general unwisdom of arming members of the more impassioned gender with clubs to be bent over beautiful heads that were surely created for more entrancing purposes.

The spectacle of pretty girls losing their tempers on a lacrosse field or rink and engaging in affrays in which words, dimpled fists and tufts of hair flew all about has come within my ken but I did not enjoy it.

Not that the girls didn't put plenty of zip into the job. They surely did! Yet I wouldn't care to see them in the prize ring, either. I may be funny about my women that way, but there it is.

Lytle admitted that there had been a "volume of interest" following his statement that "the sight of leathery-legged, flat-chested girls in sweaters and shorts, running in sprints, high jumping, throwing spears into the distance or hurling quaint-looking bits of pewter for distance in competition with men, or by themselves" made him cold and unhappy. Members of a women's softball team even sent him a hatchet with suggestions as to how best employ it.
One response, from Bobbie Rosenfeld, appeared in *Chatelaine* two months later:

Athletic maidens to arms! Andy Lytle beware! We are taking up the sword, and high time it is, in defense of our so-called athletic bodies to give the lie to those pen flourishers who depict us

not as paragons of feminine physique, beauty and health, but rather as Amazons and ugly ducklings — all because we have become sport-minded and have chosen to delve so whole-heartedly in amateur sport.

No longer are we athletes the pretty maids of yesteryear. Our perfect 36's are being ruined, our features are becoming quite "Frankensteinish" shout these croquet advocators, all because we are no longer satisfied with being just a "rib of Adam."

The modern girl is a better worker and a happier woman by reason of the healthy pleasure she takes in tennis, hockey, lacrosse, swimming, running, jumping and other sports.

The sacrifices which girls have to make to keep themselves fit are all for their good. They work better because they play better. When one sees the well-filled playing fields today, one has no fear for the future of Canadian womanhood.

The eminent Lytle recently depicted girl track and field exponents as leathery-legged, flat-chested muscle molls running around in shorts and sweaters, feebly participating in events of athletic prowess that were woeful to watch.

Now, Mr. Lytle, is that nice? I certainly cannot subscribe to that opinion. What is more pleasing to the eye than the poise and rhythmic action of the discus hurler, as she swings and sways in her circle — the rhythm of her turn and the fine grace of the poise as the platter is released to go sailing through the air? Having witnessed many a track and field meet, I can truthfully say that nowhere can one see a bevy of healthier and happier looking women than those cavorting round the track. They seem so full of life and laughter. They effervesce with vim, vigor and vitality. Their natural beauty seems to be impaired not one bit.

The trim-figured athletic girl of today can afford to smile at her seniors who solemnly prophesied a lamentable shapelessness as a result of taking part in these games. As a matter of fact, should one meet up with a party of these leathery-limbed athletes, dressed in all their "pretties," one finds that they have left none of their feminine charms behind them on the cinder path, nor has their athletic prowess in any way impaired their dancing genius.

IN THE SPRING OF 1930 Bobbie Rosenfeld, one of Canada's most famous athletes, was skating on wobbly legs. Ill with arthritis all season, she gradually regained her health and was able to help her Toronto Pats team in the annual playoff matches. Rosenfeld accompanied her team to Montreal in early April where the Pats were defeated 1–0 in a charity game by the Quebec champion Northern Electrics. The Toronto women expected to saunter in and waltz back with another victory, but the Electrics checked them into the ice and won 1–0. *Montreal Star* sports columnist Myrtle Cook reported:

> Simone Caucheon, Northern defense star, sent a sizzling shot behind Pats' goalie Annie Miller five minutes before the final whistle. The stick-handling of Miss Caucheon opened the eyes of the fans and spelled disaster for the Toronto contingent. Miller stopped shots from the stick of Caucheon that men goalies would have trouble clearing.

In the U.S. Males Decide What's Best for Female Athletes

By 1930 Canadian women's hockey was under the jurisdiction of women's athletic associations such as the Ladies' Ontario Hockey Association. Decisions were made by women. Across the border American female athletes weren't so fortunate. Nor were they as quick as their Canadian sisters to push for more female representation in athletics, despite a growing number of competitive women's teams. Men still governed female athletics. One male official of the U.S. Athletic Union declared in 1930: "The arrangement has worked satisfactorily so far and there has been no demand for a separate federation. The women prefer to remain under masculine rule."

That may have been true or merely a male chauvinist assumption. Did anyone ask the women athletes what they preferred? Only at the end of the decade did the males governing the American Athletic Union take their cue from their northern neighbours and institute female control of women's sport.

Cook said she was shocked when she saw Rosenfeld play: "To those who knew the former ability of Bobbie it was almost heart-breaking to see those famous legs wobble — for wobble they did. Bobbie gave her best but it was not a dazzling display."

In 1931 the Toronto *Telegram*'s Phyllis Griffiths called for an official playoff between Ontario, Quebec, and the Maritimes for the eastern Canada championship. It was thought such a playoff arrangement might also capture the interest of the Northern Ontario women. Although northern girls' teams seldom ventured out of the mining country to contest provincial hockey honours, it was well-known that there were many talented puck chasers among them. The Black Cats of Haileybury had just completed a successful season, meeting and defeating most of the top clubs from the mining communities.

Again in 1931 playoff arrangements were unpredictable. After Silverwoods won the Toronto championship with 1–0 and 2–1 decisions over Aura Lee at Varsity Arena, Silverwoods and the Ottawa Rowing Club agreed to meet in Ottawa for the Ontario title. But the Ottawa arena suddenly became unavailable (was it a case of men's hockey taking precedence?) and the series was abandoned. Silverwoods invited the Ottawa Rowing Club to meet them on Toronto ice, offering $100 cash and 35 percent of the proceeds, but the Ottawa girls declined. Silverwoods had been paced all season by Vida Gowland, the husky defence star, and Dot Roffey, who scored a big goal in overtime to eliminate Aura Lee.

The Silverwoods and the Preston Rivulettes, the new LOHA intermediate champions, didn't want to pack their skates away, so they hooked up in a benefit game in Galt on March 26. Funds were raised for the Rivulettes' star centre, Helen Schmuck, who was taken ill as a result of her far too strenuous athletic activities.

New teams began to make their way onto the Ontario women's hockey map in 1931. The Black Cats of Haileybury meowed their way onto the hockey circuit, while strong teams from Windsor and Little Current lost bids to play in the big league — or at least the

LOHA. Competitive women's league hockey would slowly climb to new heights, but not in 1931.

In 1932 the Preston Rivulettes, after setting some astonishing records in women's intermediate hockey, met the Toronto Varsity team in an exhibition game at Preston. The game was fast throughout, with the Preston team displaying greater speed and checking ability. The Varsity ladies weakened badly in the third period when the Rivulettes scored three quick goals to win 4–0. The Rivulettes earned a great deal of respect with the victory and talked of entering senior play (if any) the following season. It was obvious they were far too strong for the intermediate division.

Phyllis Griffiths, writing in the *Toronto Star*, enthused:

These Preston Rivulettes have a great hockey record. They have won the L.O.H.A. intermediate title for the past two years, during which they scored 92 goals to the opposition's eight. Out of 22 games, they won 21 and tied the other 0–0, and during their 13 fixtures this winter notched 59 goals to one scored by the Kitchener Wentworths, the only team to send a puck into their citadel. Not bad, not bad.

Meanwhile, in the West, the Edmonton Rustlers blanked Canmore 1–0 and claimed the western Canadian title. The Edmonton goalie was said to have registered a hockey "first." She played the complete game without having to make a single save.

Eastern women disputed the claim and dragged out some clippings from University of Toronto hockey games played years earlier. It seems that University College had a fair collection of female hockey players entered in the interfaculty league, but no goalie. The team members solved their problem by recruiting a very large young woman who was a willing volunteer with one drawback — she had no idea how to skate. Her mates had to assist her across the ice, prop her up between the pipes, and then promise her she wouldn't have much to do.

Marm Schmuck is chaired by (left to right) Hilda Ranscombe, Nellie Ranscombe, and Helen Schmuck after another title win in 1939. Hilda Ranscombe was the female player of the decade. (City of Toronto Archives)

And they kept their promise. In one game the awkward novice made three stops, in two other games she made two stops, in another game she made one stop, and in the remaining two games she made no stops at all, there being no shots on goal. Every time she released her grip on the post she fell down, and several minutes of each intermission were taken up with getting her on and off the ice. At season's end she accepted her crest as a member of the championship team and then announced she was "retiring for life."

The Preston Rivulettes enjoyed another spectacular season in 1933 and thrilled a thousand spectators with a 1–0 victory over Bobbie Rosenfeld's Toronto women's team in an eastern playoff game. Preston's big line of the Schmuck sisters and Hilda Ranscombe was particularly dangerous, but it was a fluke goal that gave Preston the title. Marm Schmuck took a long shot on goal, and Vi Gowland, in trying to clear it, knocked it into her own net.

The new champions promptly challenged the Edmonton Rustlers for the Dominion title, and dates in the West were arranged for the showdown. Preston arrived in Edmonton on Saturday, March 18, stepped right off the train, and were beaten 3–2 in the first game of the two-game goals-to-count series. The loss was a shock to the easterners — their first in three seasons. The Rivulettes and their fans blamed fatigue (after a long train ride) and lack of practice time. But the Rustlers came right back with a 3–2 victory in the second game and captured the first Dominion championship by a 4–2 margin. The third period of the second game was a wild one, with the referee penalizing six of the Rustlers and five of the Rivulettes. Edmonton's Mary Case scored the tie-breaking goal with less than three minutes to play.

Rough play didn't bother the Rivulettes. They were accustomed to it and sometimes sought it out. Team member Gladys Pitcher, reminiscing on CBC Radio in 1991, said: "There was bodychecking, too, don't kid yourself . . . if somebody hooked you, you turned around and let them have it . . . somebody might have had three stitches here and three stitches there, but what's three stitches?"

Moviegoers that week were able to see the Rustlers playing the Lethbridge team on the ice at Banff during the newsreel. It was another "first" for women's hockey.

The Rivulettes were honoured at a breakfast in Toronto on their return from the championships. They were told that during their absence a Canadian Women's Hockey Association had been formed with Miss Wyatt of Edmonton as president. In future, they were told, a final series for the Dominion title would alternate between East and West.

There was one redeeming aspect for the travel-weary Rivs. Touring the West to play Edmonton was noted in the stands — they were actually full. Fan support for women's hockey in western Canada was at an all-time high. Toronto *Telegram* sportswriter Phyllis Griffiths took note of the 2,000 spectators and wrote: "Had the game been played in Toronto, there might have been 200 attending. And even 200 is optimistic."

Toronto Star sportswriter Alexandrine Gibb had a warning for women who took their hockey seriously in 1934:

Women's hockey is just blossoming out as a Canadian-wide contest. It is too much to believe that everything will run along very smoothly at first. Rough ice is bound to be met. Conditions unexpected and unethical will also face the hockey pioneers. You must give and take in these Canadian playdowns. It is the only way they can be arranged. When the time comes that feminine sport reaches the financial standing of the C.A.H.A. then we will be able to step out and lay down some hard and fast rules for this and that playoff. In the meantime, be tolerant . . .

So tolerance and optimism prevailed, despite the fact that most team budgets were lipstick-red and scheduling mix-ups were as common as worthless stock certificates.

WHEN CANADA WON the gold medal at the World Hockey Championship in Lake Placid in 1994, Val Francis, a Toronto resident, was watching on television. When she saw me being interviewed during one of the intermissions, discussing the colourful history of women's hockey, she phoned me. She said her mother, Mrs. Fran (Crooks) Westman, had been quite a hockey star in the thirties. Her mother, in fact, had scored all of her team's goals during the 1932 season. Her University of Toronto team played two games against Queen's. The scores were 3–2 (Toronto) and 2–2. Fran Crooks scored all five goals for Toronto. Would I like to meet her? A few days later we chatted across her kitchen table.

"I played for Havergal and then the University of Toronto," she told me. "And later I helped form a good team we called the Vagabonds. I played defence, and when we practised, the coach told me to take the puck and try to stickhandle it through all the other girls. That was his idea of a good practice drill."

Mrs. Westman showed me a faded poster, an ad for a game that she had saved for more than 60 years. It advertised a game in Port Dover, Ontario, between the Vagabonds and the Port Dover Sailorettes in 1933. The poster billed Mrs. Westman as "the outstanding lady hockeyist in Ontario." Admission to the game was 25 cents for adults, 15 cents for children.

"Did you win the game?" I asked.

She sighed. "The sad thing is I never got to play in that game. . . . I was newly married then and my husband wouldn't let me go."

I was astonished. "Why not?"

"Well, there was another game to play after the one in Port Dover, and my husband felt that two games in two days was too much hockey for a woman. I'm afraid we were rather passive in those days. We tended to listen to our husbands. I'm sure I'd react differently if I was a young woman today."

"So you stayed at home, even though all the posters had been put up announcing your participation?"

"That's right. Wives weren't as outspoken in those days. It was just the way things were then."

When we discussed injuries, Mrs. Westman couldn't recall any harm from on-ice incidents. But she had a vivid recollection of a close call that took place en route to a game one night.

"We were driving to a game — it might have been to Preston for a game with the Rivulettes — when we ran into a blizzard. We could barely see

THE PORT DOVER ——————

LADIES' HOCKEY CLUB

In Appreciation of Your Support offer you the

TREAT OF THE SEASON

They will present the

TORONTO

"VAGABONDS"

An all-Star Toronto Ladies' team featuring Mrs. Westman, the outstanding lady hockeyist in Ontario.

VERSUS

PORT DOVER

(SAILORETTES)

THE ARENA, PORT DOVER

FRIDAY, MAR. 2

Game Called 8.30 p.m.

This will probably be the last game of the season. It is costing considerable to bring this team to Port Dover and the local club trust that you will come and see this game.

Adults, 25c : Children, 15c

through the windshield of our little car. Suddenly a bus came roaring out of the snow toward us. I remember the awful screeching sound as we scraped the paint off the sides of both vehicles when we came together. It's a wonder we weren't killed."

IN 1934 THERE WAS a new challenger on the scene. The Crystal Sisters hockey team, champions of the Maritimes, made their way to Montreal in late March, where they met the Montreal Maroons in what was to have been a two-game series. In the opener the Sisters played a clever game and tied the favoured Quebec champions 2–2. Myrtle Cook, writing in the *Montreal Star*, revealed that the name Sisters was tacked onto the name Crystals to identify them from a Summerside, Prince Edward Island, male team named Crystals. In her column Cook pleaded for support for the series, stating that it meant "life or death" for women's hockey.

Even if they had heeded Miss Cook, fans couldn't have supported their favourites in game two because there was no second game. The Crystals, with a splendid chance to become eastern and even Dominion champions, announced that they were broke. With empty purses, they announced, they couldn't stay in Montreal another day. They would have to return to Prince Edward Island and concede the series to the Maroons.

Parliament Hill, of all places, responded speedily to their plight, with Cabinet ministers, senators, and parliamentarians (all from the eastern provinces) gallantly chipping in to pay the players' expenses. The Crystal Sisters unpacked their skates and declared they were back in the playoffs. But it was too late. They had already been officially disqualified. For years afterward there was speculation that the Crystals would have flattened both Montreal and Preston had they been allowed to play. The Preston girls dismissed such talk as wishful thinking.

The Preston Rivulettes, after practising for a week in the thick slush that covered their natural ice rink, were standing by. They had arrived in Montreal, even though no one had told them where and when they would be playing, and were ready to tangle with the Maroons. A single game would decide the eastern title and the winner of the new Romeo Daoust Trophy.

The Rivulettes jumped into a 2–0 first-period lead and scored again in the second when, according to Alexandrine Gibb, "a Preston shot, a soft dribbler, rolled into the nets right beside Miss Wall's little tootsies. She couldn't reach it and Hilda Ranscombe was credited with the score." The final score was 4–1 for Preston. The third period was penalty-filled, and Marjorie Black of the Maroons suffered a black eye when she was hit in the face by Hilda Ranscombe's stick.

After the Maroons fell behind, many among the 2,000 fans shouted threats at the time-keeper, who refused to stop the clock during delays, even when Miss Black received her shiner. The man finally put on his coat and left the arena, declaring, "I've had enough. I'm not getting paid for this and I don't have to stand for such abuse." So for the next little while no time was kept. After the match, Preston manager Dykeman figured the teams had played a total of 71 minutes instead of the agreed-upon 60.

The Rivulettes anticipated another meeting with the Edmonton Rustlers, western Canadian champions, for the Dominion crown and the Lady Bessborough Trophy. The Rustlers had disposed of the Winnipeg Eatons 4–0 and 4–1. But those two old bugaboos, lack of finances and ice time, made a Canadian championship series impossible. So the sweet revenge that Preston wanted to taste had to be put back in the jar until 1935.

The Rustlers credited their coach and manager, Corwin Ray "C. R." Tufford, for much of their success throughout the thirties. Like the professional coaches in the NHL, Tufford stressed fundamentals and conducted fast-paced on-ice drills and blackboard sessions in the dressing room. His two daughters, Rosemary and Elenore, were the stars on his team. Joe Zeman writes:

One cold winter, Tufford parked his car outside on the street rather than in his garage in order to provide practice sessions for his girls. He cleaned the garage of all obstructions and flooded it. The team was able to practise their shooting using Tufford's garage instead of being in the frigid outdoors.

ON MARCH 26, 1935, the *Toronto Star*'s headline was: STICKS AND FISTS FLY FREELY AS GIRL HOCKEYISTS BATTLE. More and more women players, when fouled, were retaliating with a slash to the backside or a punch to the nose. Many of them were encouraged to be more aggressive by male friends at rinkside. In the spring of 1935 the Rivulettes journeyed to Summerside, Prince Edward Island, where they defeated the Crystal Sisters 5–1 in an exciting two-game, total-goals-to-count series. The Summerside girls took the ice for the second game, smarting from a 4–0 shutout in the opener. They matched the famed Ontarians stride for stride and held a 1–0 lead until Helen Schmuck scored the tying goal midway through the third period. Time ran out with the score tied 1–1.

The Rivulettes returned home and prepared for a western invasion. The powerful Winnipeg Eatons, champions of western Canada, were determined to wrest the Lady Bessborough Trophy away from the Preston women. The Eatons had tasted defeat only twice in 14 games, and they were led by Margaret Lumsden, dubbed "a female Charlie Conacher" by western sportswriters, and by Yvette Lambert. The *Toronto Star* called Lambert "the tiny French Canadian [who] has all the verve and brilliance so typical of her race." May Manson, the goaltender, was beaten only four times in nine league games and only once in four playoff battles.

Nearly 2,000 wildly enthusiastic fans witnessed the opening game in the Galt arena and were shocked at a display of rough play as the Rivulettes humbled the visitors 7–1. Sticks and fists were swung and a total of 17 penalties were called, two of them majors. Fights took place on and off the ice, with emotional fans engaging in donnybrooks in various sections of the arena. In the second period Helen Ransom of Winnipeg and Marm Schmuck of Preston dropped their sticks and gloves and exchanged a number of full-swing blows that had the crowd gasping.

Alexandrine Gibb editorialized in the *Toronto Star* the following day:

Athletic girls do not often lose their tempers in any game. They have been taught that it is very bad indeed for the boys to do it, but it is practically fatal for girls. Hockey, with a war club in your hands, is dangerous any time a player of either sex loses his head. At least the girls didn't bother with the sticks last night, although there was some wild waving of sticks around before they discarded them and went at it with their fists. Who said the hockey headaches were over? This isn't the first time there has been trouble on the feminine ice. Over at Port Dover last year when Preston visited there, there was hair pulling and plenty of it. After it was over the teams were so disgusted with themselves that they made a pact to keep the story quiet. They did. It only leaked out yesterday that a year ago there was a feminine hockey war in which even short hair got plenty of pulling and the location of the battle was Port Dover.

The lone goal scored by Winnipeg was only the fifth given up by Preston goalie Nellie Ranscombe all season.

In game two hard feelings surfaced again. There were near fireworks as the rival players carried their sticks high and indulged in butt-ending, tripping, and boarding. There were two or three near fights and a number of scowls and angry looks. In the huge crowd, estimated at 3,000, there were fans who had journeyed from as far as Montreal in the east and London in the west. The Rivulettes kept their win streak alive with a 3–1 victory and, following the match, all bitterness was tossed aside. The players from both teams threw their arms around one another at centre ice and then headed off to a banquet. Myrtle Cook McGowan, president of the Canadian Women's Hockey Association, presented the new Lady Bessborough

Trophy to the Rivulettes and also presented miniature trophies to each member of the winning club.

The Rivulettes completed their fifth year of operation in the customary way — triumphantly. Five times provincial champions, three years eastern Canadian titlists, and now Canadian champions. In those five seasons they lost but two games, both to Edmonton in 1933.

IN THE EARLY THIRTIES the Maroons of Montreal were the class of Quebec. In 1935 they went undefeated and gave up but one goal during the schedule. In the 1936 season opener the Maroons edged Les Canadiennes 2–1 in a game that came close to being tied. When the Maroons' Helen Nicholson saw rival player "Sis" Bennett poised for a shot from close in, she tossed her stick and Bennett's shot was sent astray. Nicholson was handed a 10-minute misconduct, but she said afterward: "It was worth it."

In the summer of 1993 I visited the former Maroon star in her Cornwall, Ontario, home. She is now Mrs. Fred Woltho, and at her kitchen table we pored over faded clippings and photographs of women's games played long ago. As mentioned earlier, Helen is the daughter of Big Billy Nicholson, the famous 300-pound goaltender with the old Montreal Wanderers, the renowned "Little Men of Iron." Big Bill helped the Wanderers win the Stanley Cup in 1902 and perhaps deserves Hall of Fame consideration.

Helen broke in with the senior Maroons as a 15-year-old and went on to lead her league in scoring with 11 goals and one assist in nine games. One Montreal scribe called her "the Valois Bullet." Another wrote: "Young Nicholson is the find of the year, a player with a peculiar shot that usually baffles the guardian in the net." After leading her team to nine straight victories and another undefeated season (the Maroons outscored the opposition 34–1), Nicholson and her mates ran into major postseason problems in the form of the powerful Preston Rivulettes.

The 1936 edition of the Rivulettes journeyed to Montreal and once again captured the Romeo Daoust Trophy, emblematic of the eastern Canada women's hockey championship, with a two-game sweep of the Montreal Maroons. The Maroons were brimful of confidence prior to the opening game, then skated around in confusion as the Rivulettes drove through them and around them and won 4–0. The best of the Maroons was hard-shooting Helen Nicholson and petite Dolly Moore (sister of future NHL star Dickie Moore). Montreal's Nellie Jones suffered a broken nose when she stepped in front of a sizzling shot off the stick of Gladys Hawkins. A friend rushed Jones to hospital, but when a doctor touched her nose, Jones screamed, her friend fainted, and the doctor was required to treat two patients instead of one.

The Maroons had more goals scored against them in the two-game series with Preston than they had given up in close to 40 league tilts during the previous three seasons. The Rivulettes won the Romeo Daoust Trophy as eastern Canadian champions, while the Maroons captured the Lady Brenda Meredith Trophy as Quebec titlists. Helen Nicholson was presented with the Herbie Hoare Trophy as the Quebec league's leading scorer.

In March 1937 the now-famous Rivulettes skated to their seventh Ontario women's hockey title by defeating the Stratford Maids two games to none in a playoff series. The Stratford girls were swamped in the first game 10–1, then put up a surprisingly good fight in the second game before losing 3–2.

Tempers flared in the second match, and on more than one occasion women on both teams dropped their gloves and flailed away at each other with clenched fists. Stratford's Jean Aikens tangled with Preston's Hilda Ranscombe in one first-period scrap. In the third period Preston's Marm Schmuck battled with the Maids' Jean Stirling and both drew five-minute penalties. Schmuck, with two goals, and Ranscombe were the Rivulettes' goal scorers. Sylvie Fiddie and Toots Clark replied for Stratford.

At age 15 Helen Nicholson led the Montreal Women's League in scoring. Her father was Big Billy Nicholson, a 300-pound goaltender on the Montreal Wanderers' 1902 Stanley Cup-winning team.
(Helen Nicholson Collection)

The Rivulettes anticipated a strong challenge from the West for their Dominion title. The Calgary Grills, who captured the Alberta and western Canada titles at a Banff tournament, announced they had received an offer from Maple Leaf Gardens of a cash guarantee, which would cover the expenses of a trip east. The Grills were packing to leave when their manager, Tommy Kolt, received a telegram from Montreal. It was from Myrtle Cook McGowan, president of the Dominion Women's Amateur Hockey Association and former world record holder in the 100-metre dash.

"Do you intend entering the Dominion playdowns?" McGowan asked. "If so, your Alberta branch must pay a fee of $10 due our association. Our rules provide that the western winners coming east this year must raise their own expenses which are to be charged against playoff gates. Please advise your intentions."

Kolt was stunned. He had never heard of a Dominion hockey body. He wrote back: "What Dominion Women's Hockey Association? What fee? We have our title and a guarantee from a Mr. Norris at Maple Leaf Gardens for the Canadian finals. What have you got to do with this? If you fit in here someplace, please advise me where."

McGowan notified Kolt that new rules required the visiting team from the West to pay their own way east.

Once there the home team would award them 70 percent of the gate receipts and the Dominion Association, if necessary, would pick up the balance of their expenses.

Some Calgary officials called Miss Cook's demands ludicrous and declared the Dominion Association to be a phantom organization. One said: "They didn't hold a national playoff last season and now it looks like they're not going to have one this season. It's ridiculous."

In Preston a Rivulettes' spokesman said his organization would guarantee any western challenger $400, not 70 percent of the gate. He added: "It costs about $750 to bring a team east. That's for 12 people and that should be manageable. All I know is that they'd better not delay because the ice will soon be out of the Galt arena."

There was another team anxious to challenge for the crown in 1937 — one from Winnipeg. The Preston official said: "Why doesn't Calgary pay the $10 fee to the Dominion Association,

An Expensive Title

The attendance at the Rivulettes–Maroons 1936 series was extremely disappointing, with the total gate amounting to slightly over $250. Rivulettes manager M. J. Dykeman was disgusted. "Imagine a crowd of 168 people from a city of a million citizens," he told the Montreal Star. "Then when it came to 'settling up' we were forced to accept $150 less than what we actually paid out in expenses. That was an expensive title we just won."

The Rivs, 5–2 winners on the ice, found themselves even more out of pocket after the traditional postseries party at a Montreal hotel. Assuming they had been invited as guests of the Maroons, they were surprised to be handed a bill ($5 and some odd cents each) as their share of the party costs.

Dykeman said there was little hope of a Dominion final against the western Canadian champions from Winnipeg. "The Winnipeg team offered to come east, but their manager wanted a guarantee of $800. I'm not prepared to shoulder that kind of financial responsibility."

then travel to Winnipeg and play the ladies' team there? The winner could take the gate receipts from that game and travel east to meet our Rivulettes."

But Calgary's Tommy Kolt had his dander up and demanded an investigation into the affairs of the Dominion Association. The plot thickened when a reporter, seeking a quote from the mysterious man named Norris who supposedly offered Kolt and his Calgary team $1,400 and the use of Maple Leaf Gardens, found that nobody connected with the Gardens had ever heard of Kolt.

Finally Kolt threw up his arms and said he was abandoning plans for the Grills to compete in the championship. "Even though we're not going east, I think we can legitimately claim half of the national title," he told Calgarians. By then, at least in the East, nobody was listening.

When the Dominion Women's Amateur Hockey Association persisted in demanding funds from the Calgary Grills despite scathing newspaper reports, battlelines were drawn. There were rumours of a first ever players' strike in women's hockey. The Grills refused to bow to the Dominion Association's demands while the Rivulettes began to organize a "not-desired sit-down strike with hockey sticks still in hand." A strike was averted, even though negotiations led to playdown regulations that nobody seemed to like. Teams were required to pay travel fees plus registration fees to the Dominion Association, creating more controversy and the question — should the Lady Bessborough Trophy be at stake when some of the best teams in the country couldn't afford the travel expenses necessary to compete for it?

Bobbie Rosenfeld, president of the Ladies' Ontario Hockey Association, stepped into the breach and arranged a playoff between the Rivulettes and the challengers, the Winnipeg Olympics. The first game was played in the Galt arena on April 9. The Rivulettes, off skates for three weeks, defeated the youthful visitors 3–1. Hilda Ranscombe scored two goals for Preston, and Marm Schmuck flipped in another. Maureen Gault was the outstanding player for Winnipeg. Her work was far superior to her teammates', although Margaret Topp was a whiz on the attack and came close to scoring once or twice. Years later Topp would marry a man named Smith and become the mother of a boy named Neil, who would grow up to be the general manager of the 1994 Stanley Cup-winning New York Rangers. Another forward on the Olympics' roster was Anne Shibicky, whose brother Alex would go on to a successful NHL career with New York.

Two nights later the Rivulettes retained their national title and the Lady Bessborough Trophy with a 4–2 victory over Winnipeg. This game was played before the second largest crowd (3,126) ever to grace the Galt arena. The score might have been closer had not a Winnipeg girl deflected the puck into her own net during a scramble. In the second period Winnipeg scored a goal that was disallowed because the referee's whistle had blown a split second before the puck entered the Preston net. Maureen Gault collected two of the goals for the visitors.

After the game, the girls embraced. The rival goalies kissed and their teammates followed suit, delighting the cheering onlookers. The winners were presented with the Bessborough Trophy and miniatures and there were a number of lengthy speeches by dignitaries, which were broadcast on radio throughout western Ontario.

Referee Johnston handled the game despite the objections of his mother, who thought it unmanly of him to act as an official in a feminine game. Both the referee and his assistant survived the ordeal, and later the men were seen dancing with the women from both teams. One wag commented: "There's something you'll never see in the NHL — a game official dancing with the players."

Alexandrine Gibb, covering the game for the *Toronto Star*, wrote: "The prettiest girl on the ice was Margaret Topp of the visitors. Miss Topp, 18, is not only a tip-top player but she excels as a dancer and a musician. She occasionally flicked long eyelashes covering big blue orbs at the crowd but not sufficient to injure her game."

When the gate receipts were distributed, Winnipeg received $840, the Galt arena $500, and the Preston Rivulettes $100. "Poor Preston!" Gibb wrote. "They took the short end of the hockey stick despite staging the greatest women's hockey final ever put on in Canada. But then they had the score with them, 7–3 on the round."

The following afternoon both teams attended a junior (men's) playoff game at Maple Leaf Gardens between Winnipeg and Copper Cliff. They delighted in booing the referee, future NHL president Clarence Campbell. All the errors in the game were blamed on Campbell despite his handsome features. The Preston girls were quick to recall that Campbell had handled a game they had played in Edmonton four years earlier when they suffered the first defeat in their history.

Speaker Hipel of the Ontario legislature invited the girls to the speaker's chambers at Queen's Park, following the junior tilt. Hipel's 16-year-old daughter Norma had just completed her rookie season on defence for the Rivulettes.

In 1938 a team from Ottawa, billed as "powerful and star-studded," surfaced and promised to put an end to the Rivulettes'

Margaret Topp (now Cater) starred for the Winnipeg Olympics in the thirties. She is a former showgirl and the mother of New York Ranger GM Neil Smith.

(Margaret Cater Collection)

Marg Cater Looks Back

In 1993 Margaret Topp Smith, now Margaret Cater of Don Mills, Ontario, reflected on her career with the Winnipeg Olympics.

"To rate today's women players with women of our era is like comparing apples with oranges. Can you compare the old-time male hockey players with today's? They're faster, they're bigger, they shoot harder, and they've been taught more.

"I could play as well as I did because there was a rink near our home in Fort Garry. An engineer did all of the lighting, and at night it was grand — just perfect. There were two old CNR boxcars parked on the tracks nearby for dressing rooms — one was for boys, the other for girls. Inside they had potbelly stoves.

"My dad was all for me playing hockey, of course. He used to take me to the Amphitheatre Rink . . . but only if I had my afternoon nap. He had season tickets, and I used to go and see all the games. I could name some of the players I saw — the Pettinger brothers, for instance. And the Hextalls. And the two Colvilles. I saw Turk Broda and Babe Pratt. All of them went on to the NHL.

"We won the league championship and came to Ontario to play the Preston Rivulettes. We had a tight budget, so when we left Winnipeg we made sandwiches and took them on the train. We were put up at the Preston Springs Hotel. We had to pay for our rooms, and when we got home we were short about $300. So we went around and asked merchants and other people to donate some money. I remember asking Joe Ryan of the Blue Bombers to help out, and he gave us $200. I'll never forget that.

"We got along really well with the Preston team. Hilda Ranscombe and I corresponded for years. It was rough hockey. Somebody was always getting a few stitches, but it was all part of the game.

"We had 3,500 fans show up for our games, and the three stars were interviewed on the radio. Alexandrine Gibb wanted to meet 'that big girl on defence.' It turned out to be me because I wore these big pads. But I only weighed about 115 pounds.

"Back home we had great fun playing exhibition games in Balmoral, Manitoba, and in Emerson, just over the border in the United States. Balmoral was just four corners, and there was a big open-air rink there. The lighting was terrible, and strung up to the goalposts were potato sacks sewn together — to stop the pucks. We had such fun there.

"I gave up hockey in 1939 when the war came along. Getting married to Sid [Smith] stopped all the hockey and baseball."

winning streak. The Ottawa Rangers played nine regular season games and lost only one. Norma Locke, their stellar netminder, claimed eight shutouts and gave up only one goal all season.

Alexandrine Gibb scoffed at the advance notices touting the Ottawans: "The girls are very young. They range in age from 12 to 17 years of age. That '12' is mighty young to be playing senior women's hockey. A girl of 12 is immature, lacks weight and lacks the strength necessary to make a feminine hockey star." Gibb was also annoyed that the girls had to make way for the boys when it came to arena time:

> Girls have to take the left overs. From bantams to seniors, the boys get the preference in rinks throughout the province. And when the boys' teams have completed their schedules, then the girls get the opportunity to take the ice. Even in Preston and Galt, where the girls last year drew the largest two crowds to be seen there in a decade, even there the girls must wait until the men's playdowns are all over.

With the season almost over, the Rangers discovered they were on the Preston waiting list (the Rivulettes had promised the Cobalt Marvels a playoff series), so the Ottawa girls decided to withdraw their challenge. It is also possible someone took them aside and suggested they "grow up a bit" before tackling the seasoned Rivulettes. Then the Cobalt girls, perhaps weary of waiting for confirmed playoff dates, dropped out of the hunt.

A last-minute challenge came from Prince Edward Island. Almost unheard of, the Islanders fell 5–1 in the first game in the Galt arena. The second game, won by the Rivulettes 7–1, featured a brawl involving several players. The battle began when Gladys Pitcher of Preston and the visitors' Miss McInnes collided at centre ice, then rolled about punching and kicking. Others joined in and the referee was unable to restore peace for several minutes. When the game ended and the Rivulettes once again ruled as eastern Canadian champions, all hostility was forgotten and the opposing players parted best of friends.

Islander girls often carried big chips on their shoulders, even when they played other Maritimers. When the Charlottetown Abbie Sisters met the South Kings County team one night in the late thirties, a donnybrook broke out. In the third period two rival players started throwing haymakers at each other. With Albert Gaudet, the helpless referee, in the middle of it all, the players hammered each other until a Mountie leaped onto the ice and helped restore order. After the battle, referee Gaudet handed out a brace of major penalties and thereafter kept his whistle poised for the least sign of trouble.

Ten days after Preston demolished the Islanders, the Winnipeg Olympics showed up for another crack at the Dominion title. The opening game was a shutout — for both teams. The second, called by Alexandrine Gibb "the greatest battle I have ever seen for a Canadian women's hockey title," resulted in a 2–0 shutout for Preston and a heartbreaking loss for Winnipeg. The best player on the ice was Margaret Hoban in the Olympics' goal, while Margaret Topp was the greatest offensive threat for Winnipeg. Hilda Ranscombe and Marm Schmuck scored for the Rivulettes. The Preston kid line of Dargel, Hall, and Williams was also impressive. Their ages were 14, 15, and 16.

After the game, the teams rushed to Maple Leaf Gardens in Toronto to see the St. Boniface–Oshawa Generals Memorial Cup game as guests of the Canadian Amateur Hockey Association. I was also at this game, a wide-eyed seven-year-old attending my first game at the famous ice palace. Wally Stanowski starred for the St. Boniface Juniors, and Billy Taylor, my first hockey hero, was the best of the Generals.

A new playoff plan for women's hockey was adopted in 1939. The eastern championships were eliminated and teams were matched up in what appeared to be a logical and cost-efficient manner. Quebec teams were more or less ignored because of past difficulties in getting them involved. The first playoff series involved the Preston Rivulettes and their old rivals from Winnipeg — the Olympics. The winner, finances permitting, would advance against the Maritime champions for the Dominion title.

Preston won the opening game against Winnipeg on home ice by a 3–2 score; the second game was a scoreless tie. Pauline Sweeney Koelnel, the Olympics' star left winger and a recent bride, was hospitalized with torn ligaments after she crashed into the boards feet first. The game ended with Preston's Marm Schmuck soloing down the ice and blasting the puck at May Manson — with the tiny Winnipeg goalie making a sensational save.

The Rivulettes left immediately for Charlottetown where they easily defeated the Islanders of that city 5–2 and 7–1. The defending Dominion champions were paced by the brilliant Hilda Ranscombe–Marm Schmuck–Gladys Hawkins Pitcher line, which handled most of the scoring.

Preston went through the season undefeated. Their record was 13 wins and a tie. Their record throughout the decade, during which they forged an unparalleled 348–2 win-loss tally, clearly established them as the greatest women's team ever assembled. But their reign was almost over. Rumblings of war and an uncertain future for all Canadians forced many teams — of both genders — to suspend play. A long time-out was about to begin, a hiatus that almost sounded the death knell of women's hockey.

Newfoundland's Best — the Roverines

What the Preston Rivulettes were to women's hockey in Ontario in the 1930s, the Roverines were to Newfoundland. According to hockey researcher-writer Bob White, the name Roverines was derived from the Rovers' monicker, a men's team from Bay Roberts, Newfoundland. The Roverines, comprised of young women from the ages of 16 to 18, played in a women's league for three seasons in the late thirties. In 1938 they captured the All-Newfoundland Ladies Championship.

"It was a long time ago," says Mereida Roach Murphy, who now lives in St. John's, Newfoundland. "What I remember was the good times we had playing and travelling around together. Oh, we enjoyed it a lot."

Back then there were only five teams for women in Newfoundland, but they attracted a strong following wherever they played. They would travel from town to town by train. At first the fans were intrigued by the novelty of women playing hockey, but once they saw them in action, it became obvious that these players had mastered the fundamentals and took the game seriously.

Spectators filled the small arenas to watch the women at play, and there were as many more outside "seaming" the game. "Seaming" was a term used to describe fans who watched as much of the action as possible through the cracks or seams in the arena walls. The "seamers" were those who couldn't raise the money (50 cents) to buy a ticket for the game in those Depression days.

In 1938 the Roverines went undefeated and were hailed as the finest women's team in the country. What about the Rivulettes, you say? Well, they were the finest in another country. Remember, Newfoundland didn't join Confederation until 1949.

Women's hockey took a nosedive in Newfoundland after that championship season. The Prince's Rink in St. John's burned down and the rink in Bay Roberts was closed.

The Roverines of Newfoundland in their heyday in the 1930s.

(Mereida Roach Murphy Collection)

4

When the Stickhandling Stopped

THE FORTIES AND THE FIFTIES

Dalhousie University in Halifax was one of the few Canadian universities to ice a women's hockey team in the forties and fifties. Note the figure skates on many of the players.

(Author's Collection)

DURING THE FORTIES AND FIFTIES, there was a general decline in interest in women's hockey. Many players, in the midst of World War II, shifted their priorities and entered the work force. The spread of hostilities overseas caused women players to put down their sticks and focus on family and factory duties during those anxious years when the Luftwaffe tried to crush brave Britain. Or perhaps the women players simply grew weary of trying to topple the perennial-champion Rivulettes.

The NHL, however, gamely carried on "because it was good for the nation's morale," using lineups dotted with army rejects and kids too young to serve in khaki. The Boston Bruins, for example, were so starved for talent they employed 16-year-old Bep Guidolin, the league's youngest player. Women's teams called a "time-out." They would return to the ice, they assumed, when their men returned home, when there was time once again for leisure pursuits, in short, when conditions were back to normal.

Injecting a note of optimism into the situation was the *Globe and Mail's* Bobbie Rosenfeld. In January 1940 she noted that a women's hockey tour of the United States the previous spring had drawn 22,000 fans. She pointed out that interest was still high in many communities, with towns like Owen Sound, Mount Forest, Meaford, and Thornbury all expressing a desire to join the LOHA. In the Senior B Division, Preston, Toronto Ladies, and Caledonia remained as members of the LOHA senior group. Preston defeated Toronto Ladies 2–0 in the league opener on January 15. Jean Atkinson starred for the losers, Schmuck and Ranscombe for the Rivulettes. Later Preston captured the provincial title (their 10th) with a 6–1 drubbing of Toronto.

Rosenfeld noted there would be no Dominion playoff between Preston and the Winnipeg Olympics. "The Olympics' clientele is hardly sufficient to warrant a gate-gamble series out west," she wrote, "and the Rivulettes' customer appeal has waned since the days of the jam-packed Galt arena some couple or three years ago."

The Rivulettes and the Toronto Ladies wound down their season with an exhibition game played before a full house in St. Catharines, Ontario. Rex Stimers, the radio voice of hockey for the Niagara region, became an instant convert. He said: "I went nuts over the type of hockey I saw displayed. Why, Hilda Ranscombe made plays that would put many senior (male) players to shame."

It was during this season that Alexandrine Gibb mused: "What is it that affects women hockey players that makes them play 'roughhouse' with a stick in their hands? Men are privileged characters. They fight and are admired. Girls scrap and make headlines. And tut, tuts."

As the season concluded, there was talk of a playoff series for eastern honours — the Rivulettes versus the Ottawa Rangers — and there was talk of another tour of several U.S. cities. But that was all it amounted to — talk. Nothing came of either proposal.

It became apparent that public attention was turning away from women's hockey. Men's professional hockey was becoming all the rage, and teams were building extensive farm systems to stock their rosters. It resulted in men's and boys' teams being given priority access to ice time in public arenas; the women took the ice when they could get it, usually at the worst possible hours.

It became increasingly difficult to find sponsors for women's teams. Sponsors who wished to gain a benefit from an association with hockey jumped onto the male bandwagon and put their money into a succcessful men's organization.

At the same time newspapers all but abandoned women's hockey. Sports editors and reporters became enamoured of professional sports and shifted their focus away from amateur teams and organizations, especially women's activities. There were perks to be gained from buttering up the pros — free meals and gifts, trips to other cities, All-Star game assignments and playoff junkets. Rarely did the newspapers criticize the pro sports clubs, and when they did, powerful moguls like Conn Smythe, manager of the Toronto Maple Leafs, threatened to toss their reporters out of the Gardens' press box or cut off all newspaper advertising.

Veteran sportswriter Vince Leah, in his book *Manitoba Hockey*, wrote:

> I suppose there must be a page for women's hockey in this book although it is generally agreed it is not a game for girls and such teams as basketball, field hockey, volleyball and softball are more in the feminine line. At one time a Dominion Women's Hockey Association was active but it went out of business as interest declined. Preston, Ontario claimed to have the best women's team in Canada and the Ontarians were challenged by the Manitoba champions during the brief period of enthusiasm in the 1930's.

Leah mentioned various clubs from Winnipeg during that era, including teams of the Bell Telephone System, which had its own league. He added:

> But the early novelty wore off when the girls began to play hockey without falling down every time they went for the puck, and when a Dauphin player broke her leg in a provincial final,

this also may have chilled interest in girl's hockey. Allen Rouse, who was active in hockey, soccer, and five-pin bowling, led another revival but in time the girls went back to their basketball, curling and bowling and left hockey to their men folk.

Not all women abandoned the game. In Montreal during the war years a three-team league fought for survival. One of the players in the circuit was a fast-skating mite from the Gaspé. She played the game with speed and guile and took the bumps she received without a whimper. The grit and tenacity she displayed on the ice would become her trademark and serve her well in her other chosen profession — municipal politics. Not only did she go on to gain fame as the beloved mayor of Mississauga, Ontario, but she claims to be one of the first woman hockey players who played for cash, a professional who pocketed a fiver a game and was proud of it. Her name is Hazel McCallion, and she acted as honorary chairperson of the first Women's World Hockey Tournament in 1987:

Years ago I came up from the Gaspé to take a business course in Montreal. While I was there I joined the Women's Hockey League. There were only three teams in the league and two of them were sponsored by soft drink companies. I played centre and for each game they gave me five dollars. Imagine getting paid to play the game I loved. The only problem was I had learned to play hockey on the Gaspé coast where my game was speed — I

Mississauga mayor Hazel McCallion with Darryl Sittler's daughter Meaghan at a charity game in honour of the great woman goaltender Cathy Phillips in January 1991.

(Ontario Women's Hockey Association)

was very fast — and I'd never worn all the equipment they handed me on the Montreal team. When they loaded me down with all that gear — I suppose it was necessary — I must say it slowed me down some. But I got accustomed to it and from then on I was on my way.

It was quite a strenuous game in those days, much like today. The four girls who played defence on my team — oh, my, they could hand out some pretty hefty checks. They'd knock our opponents into or over the boards. I played just two years there — in '42 and '43 — and then I was transferred to Toronto.

I got started in hockey when my brother bought me a pair of skates at Christmas when I was about four. He took me across a field to a pond and helped me put my skates on. Of course, when I stood up I fell right back down and hit my head on the ice and I began to cry. He said, "Well, Hazel, that'll be the last time you'll hit your head like that. Hold it up from now on and I'll teach you how to skate." So I listened to my brother and I learned how to skate. I remember that day so well.

When I got older I played on the town team in Port Daniel. My sister played defence on the team. She was a big, hefty girl, and boy, could she throw a check. All the other girls soon learned to stay out of her way.

All of our ice was outdoors. There were no indoor arenas then where I lived. I soon became a real fan of the game. I enjoyed following the Montreal Maroons and the Canadiens in the NHL. Every Saturday night we listened to the games on the radio.

I like Wayne Gretzky today. He's outstanding as a player and as an individual. Such a pleasant young man. Always so very friendly.

Women's hockey needs a great deal of support. I'm working with the provincial government in Ontario, and I think the biggest contribution I can make is to use the contacts I have with the people in government. I don't think women's hockey has received enough support over the years. The women who play need a lot of backing to get organized, certainly to get as well organized as the males. They need support. They can't be thrown in with the male hockey system as it is at the present time. Women's hockey needs more promotion. I'm very proud that Ontario leads the way and that Mississauga plays a major role in women's play. I'm proud of our women's hockey league in Mississauga and the wonderful growth it's shown over the years. I'm always trying to get sponsors for them. It's easy to get sponsors for male teams in minor hockey, but it's never easy to find someone to sponsor the girls.

I predicted we'd be in the Olympics someday and I'm thrilled it's going to happen. But again, we need the assistance of the provincial and federal governments in this regard. They must realize that out of all the money they set aside for hockey they've got to enrich the subsidy for women's hockey. Women can't be treated the same as the men because the numbers are not as large, and if they do it on a per capita basis, then the girls will not receive the financial support they need.

I also believe there will be a professional league for women someday — perhaps in the next 10 or 15 years. Think of it — all these skilled women competing in a professional league of their own.

If someone had asked Lynnie Grady her thoughts on professional hockey for women half a century ago, she would have laughed. Everyone in Summerside, Prince Edward Island, knew that pro hockey was for men only. Girls might be tolerated in pickup games — if teams were really desperate for players. And they could form their own teams if they wanted to — but who really cared? Had she been told there were girls in Montreal who actually received money for playing the game she would have been flabbergasted:

I played hockey back in the forties. I was Lynnie Gallant then. There simply wasn't much recreation for girls back then. Many of us girls who were interested in hockey started playing the game. That was about all there was to do in winter. We had about 20 girls involved and we played teams in Mount Pleasant and O'Leary and Charlottetown. And a team from the base, of course. There was no age limit, but most of us would be in our teens — from 13 to about 18, I would guess. We kept our team together for about four seasons. Some of us wore figure skates, but most of us borrowed our brothers' old skates. We played all of our games outdoors, so we'd wear many pairs of socks. We had shinpads and gloves and that was about it for equipment.

Not too many of us knew anything about positions. We had a coach one year who told one of the girls to go on defence. When the coach looked around for her a minute later, she was sitting on the sideboards. "What are you doing over there?" he shouted. She yelled back, "But you told me to go on the fence."

My sister Connie, who was two years older than me, got hit with the puck in a game and was knocked out. Now we used to fight a lot as sisters will and I felt real bad when I saw her lying on the ice not moving. So I knelt down next to

her and began to pray out loud, "Oh, please, God! Don't let her die. Please don't let Connie die. I'll be nice to her from now on, I promise. Just don't let her die." In a minute or two she jumped up and started playing again, and I felt kind of foolish for wailing and praying like I did.

Sometimes there was a bit of liquor involved in those games. Not with us but with some of the older girls who kept a little bottle in their hockey bags. And they'd take a little nip to keep them going. But we never did. I guess they learned that from the boys.

When the game was over we'd head for home where our folks would be waiting to hear what happened — who won and who got the goals. Mom would have some hot gruel ready for us to eat and maybe some hot chocolate.

Often the whole family would go to the game, and it always gave you a boost to hear them cheering from the sidelines. Our friends and family would get a lot more vocal whenever we played Borden because they had the roughest, toughest women's team around. If we showed up at school with bumps and bruises and cuts on our faces, the teacher would nod and say, "You girls must have been playing Borden again." We'd laugh and say, "That's right, Teacher."

In the West in the 1940s many of the colourfully named teams packed their sweaters and socks in mothballs. The Icebergs and the Snowflakes melted into oblivion, the Prairie Lilies no longer flowered, the Amazons disappeared with the Golden Gals. One team that stubbornly carried on through the war years was the Moose Jaw Wildcats. But opponents were hard to find. Women were engaged in the war effort, not organized games. By the 1950s the Wildcats were playing men's teams. They captured the Canadian women's senior title in 1951, defeating the Port Arthur Bearcats 4–0 and 8–1, and they retained their title the following year with 5–2 and 5–0 victories over the Winnipeg Canadianettes.

The Wildcats were fortunate to survive the decade. In 1940–41 in Saskatoon the Canadian army took over the Rutherford Arena and used it for training purposes. University of Saskatchewan coach Bill Wilson told Joe Zeman: "We were pushed outdoors and it was cold. We recruited a girl named McCann (later Mrs. Art Domes) to be our goalie. I remember the first shot that sailed in higher than her waist knocked out her two front teeth. She left the ice and was never seen again."

In the mid-forties some students organized a 10-team coed league at the University of Toronto, but if the players expected to earn the respect of the sportswriting fraternity, they didn't get it — at least not from the *Toronto Star*. Reporter Lloyd Lockhart showed up one day with a photographer in tow. While the photographer coerced the best-looking girls to pose with compacts and powder puffs, Lockhart used words like "oomph" to describe the circuit. Then he focused on the uniforms of the day:

> The majority of co-eds favor shorts and no stockings, the theory being stockings cut down one's velocity, if you can figure that out. Most girls wear sweaters but some like rolled up sleeves. Ribbons are very popular. The right shade of ribbon draws a bigger hand from the gallery (men, remember?) than a girl who can raise the puck. Past records show Victoria College usually wins the championship and this leads some players to question Vic's ethics and even to impute the league leaders import "ringers" from Northern Ontario.

> "Don't breathe a word of this," a husky blonde said in the corridor, "but some of their players were offered extra telephone facilities if they enrolled at you-know-where."

> A good fraction of the girls wear figure skates — a sight not calculated to stir Leaf owner Conn Smythe's contract-signing tendencies. Even the goalkeepers wear figure skates, claiming the curved blades give keener balance. Goalie Turk Broda of the Leafs was asked if he would like to

wear figure skates and Mr. Broda retorted, "You figure it out." Sitting behind the player's bench at a girl's hockey game is a shattering experience. All members of the other team, it soon develops, are "big bruisers." The referee is a "dumb cluck" and a very much overused word is "smear."

"I'm going to smear that blonde," said one girl.

"Which blonde?" said another.

"You know," said the first. "The one who dyes her hair, wears purple nail polish, plucks her eyebrows and goes with that drip in med."

So much for coed hockey, concludes Lockhart.

Elimination of interscholastic sports was another factor in the demise of women's hockey in the postwar years. Curtailment of interschool match-ups, which began in the thirties, carried over into the fifties and sixties. The cutbacks didn't dramatically affect boys. There was an abundance of minor hockey leagues, little league baseball, soccer, and football programs for them. But similar opportunities on the playing field simply didn't exist for their sisters. It is amazing that young Canadian women, given the obstacles they had to overcome, rose to the top in any sport. But many did, particularly in winter sports like figure skating and skiing.

One who became a world-class athlete in track, and a two-time Olympian, first became aware of the obvious discrimination against her sex when she was only eight years old and an aspiring hockey player. Even at that young age Abigail Hoffman decided to fight the system.

In 1955 Hoffman took a hard look at organized hockey and decided that girls weren't getting a fair chance to participate. She played hockey with her brothers at the corner rink and figured she was just as adept with puck and stick as the boys in her age bracket. In fact, she was better than most of them.

So Abby registered as a player in the Toronto Hockey League. The official who checked her birth certificate assumed she was a male. He said, "Get your skates on, Ab, and go out and practise."

For the rest of the season Abby Hoffman became "Ab" Hoffman. Abby's parents decided not to say anything, even though it was obvious the league was for boys only. Abby was anxious to prove she belonged, and they kept their silence.

How pleased they were when Abby turned out to be a star defenceman. Her coach said, "I want Ab on defence because he hands out solid checks and plays a rough game." Later, when Abby's secret was out, the coach said he was amazed to discover that Ab was a girl.

Near the end of the season the league selected an all-star team, and Ab Hoffman was a unanimous choice. It was then that league officials checked all the birth certificates a second time. Someone phoned Mrs. Hoffman and said, "Ab must have brought in his sister's birth certificate by mistake. The one I have is a girl's."

Only then did Abby's mother explain the whole story. Suddenly the entire sports world showed an interest in the young hockey star. Her story made headlines everywhere, and there were features about her in magazines and on television. She was invited to see an NHL game at the Montreal Forum as a guest of the Montreal Canadiens, and a sports reporter took her to a game at Maple Leaf Gardens.

Abby continued to play with her team, but there was a difference. She was given her own dressing room. "I think I'm the only player in history to have my very own room," Abby once said, laughing.

The next season Abby was persuaded to play on a girls' hockey team, but the league had difficulty setting up a schedule, so Abby decided to quit the game and turn to other sports. She became a swimming champion and a track star. By age 15, after only a year of training, she was the top Canadian woman in the 880-yard run.

Within months she was ranked as one of the fastest runners in the world in her event. She competed in the Commonwealth Games and in two Olympic Games. In Munich, in 1972, she failed to win the gold medal in the 800 metres but finished a mere second behind the winner. Her time — a remarkable 2.00.02 — was the fastest time of her career and faster than the previous Olympic record.

When she retired from athletics, Abby became director of Sport Canada in Ottawa. In 1973, reflecting on her life as an athlete, she talked with Anita Latner of the *Toronto Star* about the sexual chauvinism that figured prominently in sports at that time.

Called "Ab" by her coach and teammates (see name on stick), Abby Hoffman became the first female player to create a sensation by starring in a boys' league in the 1950s. Many of Abby's girlfriends were figure skaters.

(Author's Collection)

On hockey: "When I was thrown off the boys' team, I just accepted it because girls didn't play hockey. We all did but, being girls, we were just supposed to figure-skate. The irony is girls complement men on the ice. Where men tend to be stronger skaters because of their physiology, women are naturally more agile and flexible."

On track: "I remember being thrown off the track at the University of Toronto because women weren't allowed in. It was the only track available and I needed to train."

On women in sports: "Girls are fed up with being restricted to cheering. They want to actively participate in sports. Sports in school is geared for boys. That's where the bulk of the money goes. Boys' football teams rate all-day pep rallies while girls' volleyball teams go unnoticed. If women are stupid enough to accept the theory that they are weaker than men, more passive than aggressive, stupid rather than intelligent and consequently not supposed to participate in sports, they deserve to be treated as they are being treated in sports today — as second-class citizens. There aren't any female coaches, administrators, heroes, or sportswriters. And there's a lack of opportunity and little encouragement for a girl to enter sports. If a girl is exceptional, she's accepted as an athlete. But if she's just average, she's questioned as to why she's trying to be like a man."

Speaking from the heart, Abby verbalized what other young women were thinking. Many of the "second-class citizens" she referred to would find the courage and the confidence to demand more participation in sport — and much better treatment — in the decades to come.

5

The Excitement Returns

THE SIXTIES AND SEVENTIES

THE SIXTIES SAW WOMEN'S HOCKEY undergo a revival as teams and leagues returned to arenas across the land. There was a resurgence of interest in intercollegiate play, especially in Ontario, where female students at Queen's, Western, the University of Toronto, and the Ontario Agricultural College (now the University of Guelph) lobbied their institutions for financial support. In Montreal students at McGill iced a team to compete against the Ontario women.

Women's teams were organized in British Columbia early in the decade, the first evolving from a softball team whose players wanted to play a sport during the winter months. Interior and northern B.C. teams sprang up and exchange trips soon resulted.

In 1963 Preston, Ontario, home of the renowned Rivulettes in the thirties, iced a new team featuring an old star. The Preston Golden Trianglettes was formed late in the 1963 season. In the lineup was a female counterpart of Gordie Howe — Hilda Ranscombe. She had led Preston to hockey glory throughout the thirties.

Molson's sponsored this women's team in Montreal in 1962. Although their uniforms now look more like those worn by their male counterparts, most of the players are still wearing figure skates.

(National Archives of Canada)

Many of the players were now outfitted in black stretch slacks with equipment worn on the outside. Midway through the decade players began donning full hockey equipment comparable to the male style, and white skates had all but disappeared. Still, the world of women's hockey had its detractors. One of the most notable was writer Scott Young, who penned an article entitled "Does Your Sweetie Have a Charlie Horse?" Young later became a booster of women's hockey when he wrote a history of the Ontario Hockey Association.

By 1964 the Brampton Canadettes, organized by Roy Morris, set standards for other organizations to follow. Morris, with the support of others, including Marg Poste and Joan Connell, was responsible for the first youth house league for females in Ontario. On the four teams involved he colour-coded players' helmets so that lines were changed according to age and ability. The Canadettes organization established the Dominion Ladies Hockey Tournament in 1967, a centennial project that would have far-ranging consequences. From the 22 teams that entered the three-division inaugural tournament, the Brampton event has blossomed into the largest female hockey tournament in the world, encompassing 258 teams in 25 divisions in 1994. Other tournaments in the sixties were staged in many communities across Canada, but with the majority in Ontario. Julie Stevens, in her thesis on the women's game, states:

> For many women, these events were the highlight of the season since they were able to play against other women of the same level. The tournaments enhanced the development of women's hockey in two ways. First, they provided a meeting place where enthusiastic people within the hockey community could exchange ideas. Second, as more girls became involved in the game, the tournaments expanded to include younger age categories and enhanced participation at both youth and adult levels.

In 1967 a small-town recreation director and his wife decided to draw attention to their community through a hockey tournament. Harold and Lila Ribson of Wallaceburg, Ontario, organized the Lipstick Tournament for female players, a three-day event that proved to be enormously successful and attracted more than 400 competitors. It also proved to be a boon to local merchants in the town of 10,000.

A special guest of the tournament — the tournament queen, if you will, was Jean Walker, 81, of Chippewa, Ontario. Miss Walker, a former goalie for St. Hilda's College in 1904, said the greatest problem for women when she played the game was prejudice against female teams. "I guess there is still some, but I'll bet there were some proud old grandfathers watching today who don't feel the same now as they did then."

Fans who turned up for the playoff game between two Toronto teams, Islington and Don Mills, were of the opinion that both teams would be capable of defeating a few of the men's teams competing in the area.

As a young broadcaster back then, I joined several of my *Hockey Night in Canada* colleagues and travelled on a chartered bus to Wallaceburg to film a portion of the tournament — and to take part in an abbreviated exhibition game against the Wallaceburg Hornettes. The broadcasters' starting line of McFarlane, Bill Hewitt, and Ward Cornell received a rude welcome from the Hornettes. At the opening whistle I was tossed to the ice by a husky Hornette winger, Hewitt lost the face-off and was unable to gain possession of the puck in the two-minute chase that followed, and Cornell, stunned by the speed and aggressive nature of the Wallaceburg girls, made survival his top priority. He headed for the sideboards, clung to them for support, and greeted each passing Hornette with a wink and a cry of "Go, girl, go!"

Later, when Hewitt snared the puck and raced in on goal, he was tackled from behind by Roxann McFadden. When he protested, she gave him a peck on the cheek and the referee gave him a two-minute penalty for "having lipstick on his collar." The hockey announcers didn't have a chance and the Hornettes won 6–2.

The Toronto Humberside Dairy Queens defeated the Don Mills Satan's Angels 2–1 to capture the first edition of the North American Girls Hockey Championship. Cookie Cartwright broke up the contest with a breakaway goal at 11:20 of the final period, while stellar netminding by Pat Nicholl caught the eye of the large crowd.

Both Nicholl and Cartwright were singled out by Jack Adams, then Detroit Red Wing general manager, and Johnny Mowers, former Red Wing goaltender, as the top performers. "They're using a lot more brains in this tournament than a lot of the players I've managed over the years," Adams cracked.

There was only one sourpuss in attendance — reporter Dave Agnew of the *Chatham Daily News*. He wrote:

Girls, girls, girls — who needs them? Certainly not the sport of hockey. And yet these feline pretenders seem determined to take over every last vestige of the once proud male domain. Women, who once took pride in making a home for their children and their male counterparts, are now pursuing their own careers in the worlds of business and finance — also at one time belonging only to the male.

And as they exert their feminine wiles over disgruntled males, they gradually move into every nook and cranny of his realm and at the same time rob him of what is left of his ego.

Last weekend a coup was attempted on another of the exclusive male pastimes. Hundreds of girls took over stock and barrel, to stage what was called the "North American Girls Hockey Championships." Now this is all well and good for it was all taken in a less than serious vein: unfortunately the tournament itself was most serious. The girls played as if they had a future in the sport. If it is possible to project into the future one can imagine a typical Saturday night. Instead of the husband getting together with a few of his cronies at the local pub to view the

Canadiens and Leafs fighting it out, he remains at home where the wife forces him to watch the Burlington Buffaloettes and the Kapuskasing Kookettes match wits in a hockey game.

And fight they do. The John Ferguson knock-out punch no longer livens up a dull game. Instead women check each other senseless, pull each other's hair and even take a crunching bite every once in a while. After the game some little girl timidly approaches her idol girl hockey player and asks for her autograph. The hockey star smiles at the toddler and suddenly her false teeth fall out on the floor. The once attractive feminine figure is no more. The calorie intake necessary to produce the desired amount of energy just doesn't agree with the waistline. Soon protruding muscles cover her body. But no matter how far one looks into the future, it is unlikely that the gals will ever triumph. Harold Ribson, who promoted the tournament in Wallaceburg, mentioned that the University of Toronto had a girl's hockey team in 1904. And they haven't managed to gain control yet.

HAROLD AND LILA RIBSON were true pioneers and outstanding boosters of women's hockey. When Harold was recreation director and arena manager in Lucan, Ontario, in 1956, he organized a peewee team — the Lucan Leprechauns. Lila named the team and designed the uniform. Harold's next step was to get some publicity for his team, which featured a forward line of three gifted young women. He and Lila wrote Ed Sullivan in New York, never expecting an answer. They told Sullivan, host of the most-watched show on American television, about their team and the need for a little recognition. Sullivan not only answered the letter but invited the Leprechauns to appear on a forthcoming show. The Ribsons immediately set about raising $600 — the amount of money it would take to get to New York. A faded photograph in the Ribsons' collection, taken on St. Patrick's Day, 1958, reveals the cherubic faces of their Leprechauns smiling self-consciously at the cameras while a grinning Ed Sullivan hovers in the background. The photo made the front page of the *Toronto Star*.

The Leprechauns were good enough for Ed Sullivan — they were even invited to be part of New York's famed St. Patrick's Day parade — but they were less welcome at home with the Canadian hockey establishment. The Leprechauns' female forward line was banned from competing in the provincial championships that season. No girls allowed was the verdict.

Everywhere the Ribsons went, they established more women's teams and fought for more ice time and more recognition. Often they received more ridicule than recognition.

"It was difficult," Lila says. "Nobody took us very seriously. But then women have never been given a break when it comes to anything athletically."

Another time, when Ribson supervised women's hockey in Cobalt, Ontario, there was talk of a player strike in the NHL. Ribson wrote NHL president Clarence Campbell and offered the services of his Cobalt Silver Belles as substitutes for the NHLers. The Silver Belles, aged 14 to 19, were using Russian training methods, claimed Ribson, and the Belles were "the best students of hockey I know and play better positional hockey than men. Not only that, but they are stunningly pretty. They typify the good looks of Northern Ontario women."

Campbell declined the offer but added an interesting paragraph in his letter of reply:

I am sure you are aware that some coaches refer to some players as "performing like girls" but from my own personal experience of women's hockey, I can't think of anything more violent or dangerous. Some forty years ago I refereed two women's hockey games in Western Canada and I consider myself to be very fortunate to escape with my life and I was equally surprised to find that all of them did likewise. I abstain from any reference to the language employed. It was in the best dockyard tradition.

"Women's hockey has always been popular," Ribson says. "I've got a picture of women playing ice hockey on a frozen pond in Wimbledon, England, in 1893. Canada has had terrific women players for decades. The trouble is, until recently it was never very well organized."

Speaking to *Calgary Herald* sports editor Hal Walker in 1973, Ribson said: "Women's hockey is flourishing in Montreal. They have two leagues and the competition is so keen that teams have been accused of stealing players from rival teams. These girls' teams make quite a few excursions into New York State during the season and on average come home with about $1,700. On the strength of that someone wrote me recently and asked me to help start a pro league for women. But I'm too busy with other matters to get involved at this time."

Twenty years later, when I visited Harold and Lila in their Ottawa home, he was still not interested in getting involved in a pro league. At age 80 he was in retirement. But he did predict such a league. "The day will come when women will be playing hockey professionally."

When asked to name the best female player he ever saw, there was no hesitation. "Hilda Ranscombe, star of those great Preston Rivulettes teams in the thirties, was the best." He also named Charlotte Whitton, a player with Queen's and a former Ottawa mayor, as an outstanding college player.

Dᴜʀɪɴɢ Cᴀɴᴀᴅᴀ's ᴄᴇɴᴛᴇɴɴɪᴀʟ ʏᴇᴀʀ — 1967 — women's hockey thrived in Montreal and teams were organized in other Canadian cities. In addition, universities in Quebec and Ontario budgeted for women's teams.

In Montreal's east end the Aces Hockey League attracted a mix of French- and English-speaking players. A deck of cards supplied the team names — Hearts, Spades, Clubs, and Diamonds — and one of the problems was impending motherhood.

"We have lost a few players because of pregnancies," Françoise Janneau, a league official, said. "But it's not a major problem. Most of the girls are young and single and not ready for babies."

A bigger problem for the Aces League was player pilfering. A rival league, playing out of Paul Sauvé Arena, began luring the star players from the Aces League to the new circuit, and hard feelings resulted. There were accusations that officials of the new league were paying players to join their teams. "We try to protect ourselves by having players sign contracts and get player cards from the Quebec Amateur Hockey Association," Janneau said. "Our rules are a combination of standard amateur regulations and the Olympic rules. We don't allow rough stuff and, being women, I think we would be crazy to try it. We stick to pretty basic hockey."

Teams in the Aces League were sponsored and fully equipped. At the end of the season trophies were presented to the regular-season and playoff champions. Other awards went to the top scorer, the best goalie, the top defender, and the most valuable player.

At one point in the season two of the clubs journeyed to Manchester, New Hampshire, to play exhibition games. "Our purpose was to get young American girls interested in hockey," Janneau said. "Many of them came to see us play and said they would like to take up the game."

"People used to laugh, especially the men, when they heard about our league," Janneau added. "They would promise to come to one of our games and laugh some more. But when they did show up, there was no laughter. They stopped treating us as a joke and they had to admit we were pretty darn good."

KATHERINE "COOKIE" CARTWRIGHT was at the peak of her playing career in 1967. She had been a star at Queen's on a team she organized herself. But let her tell the story.

"It's true we started our own team at Queen's in 1961. We had to persuade the director of athletics it was a good idea. You see, there were only seven sports women could participate in at the university in those days and hockey wasn't one of them. The athletic director was a lady named Marion Ross, so I went to her when I was a freshman, all bright-eyed and bushy-tailed, and pushed hard for intercollegiate hockey. We already had intramural hockey, and Miss Ross thought that was quite enough.

"Perhaps you've noticed that people tend to treat female hockey players like oddballs. Hockey was kind of an oddball sport for women to play. It attracted players who would not normally play intercollegiate sports — like the phys ed students. So gradually Miss Ross was swayed and got to like the idea. Then came the matter of a budget. Miss Ross asked me how much I thought intercollegiate hockey would cost, and I convinced her it wouldn't be too much. If she was up on what was happening at the other universities, she knew that McMaster, McGill, and Toronto all had women's teams. They had budgets.

"Miss Ross still didn't say yes. She wanted to know how much equipment would cost and where we thought the money for it would come from. I didn't know, of course, but I stalled her for a while until I could deal with this problem.

"Now the old stadium at Queen's was a huge barn with seats. And underneath those seats were the dressing rooms. All the dressing rooms connected one to another, but there were two that were always used. One day the team trainer said to me, 'Cookie, come with me. I think I may be able to help you.' He took me under the seats, through a couple of dressing rooms, and into a third, run-down old room and started opening all these boxes. Inside he found shin-pads, elbow pads, and some old hockey pants — equipment that had been stored in there since the thirties. All packed in mothballs. I was delighted. Now Miss Ross had no reason not to let us play. So she conceded. We played exhibition games for a couple of years and then we became a full-fledged collegiate team.

"After college I discovered the Humberside Omegas in Toronto and I played for them. There were other teams in Toronto and in Burlington, Barrie, and Oshawa. And in Scarborough Harry Lazerenko helped women's hockey enormously. He set up a farm system for his Senior A team there. It was the best team around in 1960. Harry passed away in the early seventies.

"There were little hotbeds of women's hockey around the province — in places like Guelph and Pembroke. Hockey was big in the small towns then, but now it's more in the big cities.

"For the 1969–70 season we decided to start up our own team in Kingston, a team we called the Red Barons. And we were good! Annabelle Twiddy was a star on that team — one heck of a hockey player. She came from a small town near Trenton, a place called Stockton, where her father owned a sawmill. One year Annabelle scored 52 goals in 13 games.

"There were six of us who had played some hockey, and a lot of the others were basketball players who made the switch to the ice game. Debbie Murray, Rhonda Leeman, Barb Campeau, and Pat Fowler made the switch with amazing ease. We played in the Picton League against teams from Picton, Belleville, Peterborough, Napanee, and Cobourg. We had a good first season but lost to Peterborough in the finals.

"In the Ontario championships that year we defeated a strong Toronto entry, Litton's Canadettes, 2–1 but were outclassed by one of my former teams, the Lambton Ladies. The Lambton coach said he was amazed at how well we played considering that several of our players had never played hockey before. He singled out Kim Ferguson for special praise. She was our 12-year-old winger whose positional play throughout the year had taught many older players how to perform.

"Kim was the daughter of former NHL player Lorne Ferguson. Later she played on our 'Kid Line' with two other girls whose fathers were deeply involved in hockey. One was Sue Scherer, daughter of Kingston Canadians general manager Walter 'Punch' Scherer, and Janean Gerow, daughter of Napanee Comets' coach Walt Gerow.

"Little Kim joined us when she was just 10 years old. She was the classic, ignored player in her family. She played with cast-off equipment from her brothers. I don't think her parents ever bought her new equipment. She even played for some time in a pair of skates with a big hole in one of them so that part of her foot stuck out. Poor thing. I remember there was a fight

on the ice one time. Kim dropped to the ice and put her hands over her head until it was over.

"Fights never bothered Sue Scherer, who had grown up watching the Junior A style of hockey. Her father had coached Junior A, so that's how she played — carry your stick high and take the offensive. Sue was . . . well, handy with her stick, let's just say. Handy at hooking and spearing. It took us a couple of seasons to reeducate her.

"One time the Massport Jets, an American team, came up from Boston to take us on. All of the Boston players kept their sticks high. They'd been watching the Boston Bruins on television and played like the Bruins did. They were cross-checking and high-sticking us and we were getting tired of it, even though we were winning handily — by about 7–2, I think.

"Then one of them took a punch at Sue, and Sue, being the best street fighter on our team, turned around and decked her. With that, all the Boston players tried to pick a fight with the Kingston player closest to them. But the rest of us weren't like Sue. So we were saying things like, 'What are you doing?' And we didn't fight. But Sue did. So all these Boston girls are swinging at us and we're trying to get away from them. But not Sue. She stood there and dished it out to anyone who came near her.

"The Red Barons always played clean hockey — really clean. Ask anybody who saw us play. The intercollegiate game had a "no intentional bodychecking" rule at the time, while the Senior A league adopted regular rules, so there were adjustments to be made. A few of the playoff games in the Senior A in Toronto were a bit wild. One night my nose was spread all over my face — with only 10 minutes to play — by a Satan's Angel. I don't know why she bothered, because we were about to lose the game, anyway.

"One year we established ourselves as the number one Senior A team in Ontario, and we swept the North American Championship at Wallaceburg. We were very solid on defence, thanks to Sue Wright, who was everybody's choice as the outstanding female hockey player in Canada in 1973. And she kept getting better. Even now, some 20 years later, I believe Sue Wright could make the national team. Why, she'd be head and shoulders better than anyone on the nationals.

Manitoba's Starettes on First Broadcast of Women's Hockey

On November 22, 1975, radio station CJRB in Boissevain, Manitoba, aired the first play-by-play account of a women's hockey game. The announcer was Dwight McCauley and the game, played in Souris, was between the Goodlands Starettes, champions of the Westman Girls' Hockey League, and an all-star team selected from member clubs in Elkhorn, Pierson, Souris, Brandon South, and Brandon East End.

"We have checked with the CAHA in Ottawa and they had to admit they'd never heard of a girls' hockey game being broadcast in Canada," said McCauley prior to the historic event. "When the game is over, I plan to send the CAHA a letter or tape of the game informing them our station has done it. With 1975 being International Woman's Year what better time could there be for such a broadcast to take place?"

The Starettes won the game, and Barb Lumsden (neé Austin) was one of the goal scorers. Now living in Sparwood, British Columbia, Barb has many fond memories of her hockey-playing days with the Starettes. "Most of us wore figure skates initially," recalls Barb, "and we played body contact. By 1977 we had all switched to men's skates for safety reasons, and by 1982 'no body contact' was the rule. We won the league title for seven straight seasons, and the league survived for 14 years."

"In goal at that time we had Wanda Gyde, a real steal from Picton. Wanda used to say that if she survived the practices, with Sue Wright and Janean Gerow blasting pucks at her, the games that followed were easy. Both had tremendous shots, and Janean was often called 'Boom Boom' Gerow in the papers."

In 1974 Cookie dashed off a letter to the American Hockey Association, supporting a bid for women's hockey to be included in the Olympics:

> We in Canada are envious to see the American Girls Hockey Association with the organization and the enthusiasm necessary to achieve that goal; we are also monumentally ashamed to realize that we, in the birthplace of hockey, are lagging so badly behind the United States.
>
> Historically, hockey in Canada flourished among ladies in the 1920's, and in fact ranked only slightly behind men's hockey at the time, both in terms of numbers of participants and enthusiasm generated among sports followers. If the ideal of equal opportunity had extended then to women, hockey would undoubtedly now be an accepted Olympic sport for women.
>
> The obvious tremendous boost that an Olympic team would give to the sport is beyond imagination. At the same time, I believe that the girls would maintain ideals of pure amateurism, that is, participation for the love of the sport and not for material rewards of any kind. As you are no doubt aware, several years ago, Canada was seriously questioned as to the amateurism of its hockey players and, as a result, the men withdrew from Olympic competition. But the girls and young ladies are true amateurs within the Olympic code.
>
> Having been involved in ladies' hockey in Ontario for approximately fifteen years, I feel qualified to speak for at least one thousand Canadian girls and young women, in advocating the entry of ladies' hockey into the Olympics, for the betterment of hockey in general, for the

encouragement of an increasingly large body of young people, be they only female, and for the boostering of the Olympic ideal, at a time when it is badly in need of reinforcement.

In 1974 only a woman with phenomenal powers of clairvoyance could envision an Olympic tournament for females on the hockey horizon. Cookie Cartwright possessed such powers. At the same time, as a realist, she knew it might be decades before women players stickhandled their way into the Olympics. She recognized that most members of any Olympic organizing committee — almost all of them men — were less than enthusiastic about stick-wielding women crashing into each other on Olympic ice. They looked on hockey for females as a bloody and bruising "sweat" sport — decidedly "unfeminine." Besides, they argued, adding another team sport to an already crowded Olympic agenda was costly. Would anyone pay to see them play?

As women's hockey grew throughout the 1970s, informal discussions regularly revolved around the value and feasibility of forming a unified organization within Ontario. On September 6, 1975, a meeting was held in Toronto with provincial government consultant Jim Coutts, and the Ontario Women's Hockey Association was born.

The OWHA was incorporated in 1978 and was accepted as part of the Ontario Hockey Council in 1979, then became a member of the Ontario Hockey Association the following year. With support from the Ottawa District Hockey Association, the OWHA was given jurisdiction for all ages and ability levels of female hockey in the province — a unique mandate in Ontario.

As Fran Rider, the executive director of the OWHA, says, "The OWHA is the only organization of its kind in the world, since it is totally structured and dedicated to the development of female hockey." According to her, the "existence of the OWHA, with its strong support and special partnership with the Ontario government and male hockey bodies in the province, has been a key factor in the provincial, national, and international advancement of the game. The OWHA has domestic hockey programs for fun, friendship, and fair play, which are the major objectives.

However, it has also been very active in lobbying for the inclusion of women's hockey in organized competition at all levels, from the Ontario Winter Games to the Olympics."

If proof was needed that women's hockey was on the rise, it would come in the eighties in the form of national and world championships, ultimately forcing a welcome shift in attitude among the Olympic organizers.

6

Better, Faster, Bolder

THE EIGHTIES

Team Canada wins the first world tournament for women hockey players in Mississauga, Ontario, in 1987. Mayor Hazel McCallion presents the cup named after her to captain Marion Coveny (left) and goalie Cathy Phillips.

(Ontario Women's Hockey Association)

I N THE EIGHTIES the federal government placed a new emphasis on opportunities for women in sport, and a series of seminars, begun in the late seventies, were held to determine the status of women's hockey in Canada. With the inaugural Shoppers Drug Mart Women's National Hockey Championship in Brantford, Ontario, in 1982, female hockey, for the first time, received full national attention. In May 1982 the Canadian Amateur Hockey Association established a female hockey council — another first. The Ontario Women's Hockey Association's past president Frank Champion-Demers recalls the events that led up to the breakthrough:

The OWHA, after consultation with the female provincial representatives, took on the task of organizing the first Canadian National Women's Hockey Championship. Abby Hoffman and Maureen McTeer were quickly recruited to spearhead the operation. These two Canadian personalities provided the credibility needed with the press, as well as hockey and government representatives.

The OWHA seconded their full-time development coordinator to provide the administrative support needed. The Brantford female hockey association provided the venue, the volunteers, and the municipal cooperation that was needed to ensure success. The OWHA executive became close to full-time workers, as well. Finally Shoppers Drug Mart and Sports Canada provided the sponsorship and funding to carry off this first Championship, thus reviving the tradition that had been established in the twenties to hold East–West championships on a yearly basis.

At the conclusion of this initial championship the first female council was formed, and after a close vote, the council was welcomed with difficulty into the CAHA male bastion. Fortunately, with the passage of time and the acceptance of female hockey by the Olympics, the council has increased its profile within the CAHA.

The OWHA also took the initiative and organized the first world tournament in Toronto. This led to the International Ice Hockey Federation's approval of the first Women's World Championship in Ottawa in 1990. And, within Canada, the Canadian winter games and Ontario winter games now include women's hockey.

Thanks largely to the efforts of the OWHA it was anticipated that more than 500 teams and over 10,000 players would register with CAHA branch associations. Without a doubt women's hockey was now a force to reckon with.

At the press conference prior to the initial Shoppers Drug Mart Women's National everyone chuckled, including Maureen McTeer, when Toronto Maple Leaf VP King Clancy called the former prime minister's wife "Mrs. Joe Clark." And they laughed when Abby Hoffman, whose name was on the championship trophy, quipped, "I thought you had to be dead to have a trophy named after you." A few months later the Abby Hoffman Cup was officially inducted into the Hockey Hall of Fame. Curator Maurice "Lefty" Reid said: "We are privileged to have the opportunity to display for the first time in the Hockey Hall of Fame a trophy of national significance for women's hockey."

Maureen McTeer, who first picked up a hockey stick when she was four years old, said she once aspired to a career in the NHL until she realized the "doors were not open to me. It's a lucrative career that women don't have access to. When I was a young girl, there weren't enough boys to make up a team, so I was *allowed* to play," she added with a grimace.

The tournament was sanctioned by the Canadian Amateur Hockey Association. All players entered were at least 18 years old with no set maximum age. Player agent Alan Eagleson helped launch the tournament, saying, "If I was a woman, I'd be a little bored to see only men involved in high-quality levels of sport. Look at what some of my clients have done, women like Cindy Nicholas, the best swimmer in the world, not just the best female swimmer, but the best swimmer. Then there's Susan Nattrass, winner of the Lou Marsh Trophy as Canada's top athlete. Nancy Greene's gold medal in 1968 is comparable to what Steve Podborski did in skiing. And Karen Magnussen — her accomplishment in winning a world title is as impressive as Donald Jackson winning one."

Asked if he thought women's hockey would ever reach the skill level and fan interest of the NHL, he said, "No, but then who would have thought that women's skiing was going to compete at the level of men's skiing? And who would have thought that a woman swimmer could compete against the best of the men?"

Shirley Cameron, a 29-year-old letter carrier from Edmonton, risked losing her job by appearing at the inaugural Shoppers Drug Mart tournament. She didn't bother to ask her boss for a leave of absence because the last time she did he turned her down. So she called in sick and hightailed it for Brantford. She looked the picture of health as she scored seven goals and eight assists for her team — the Edmonton Chimos — in the first six games in which she played.

"Sure I may not have a job when I get back home," she said, "but this was too important to pass up. At my age who knows if I'll ever get to play in the nationals again."

One of the pre-tournament favourites, the Edmonton Chimos had registered 19 wins and a tie in their 20-game schedule. A western powerhouse for a dozen years, the Chimos had captured the Western Shield four times and placed first in the Wallaceburg Lipstick Tournament and second in the nationals in 1982. A western official noted that Alberta had experienced a 35 percent increase in registration in the past year.

The Agincourt Canadians, representing Ontario, beat Cameron's Chimos 3–2 in overtime to win the first Shoppers tournament. Goalie Cathy Phillips was named MVP for Ontario, Dawn McGuire for the Chimos. After skipping a tennis match to play in the final, Ontario's Lynda Harley scored the winning goal.

Abby Hoffman (left) and Maureen McTeer present the Hoffman Cup at the first Shoppers Drug Mart Women's National held in 1982.
(Doug Perry)

During the regular season, goaltender Phillips was almost perfect. She compiled 43 victories and suffered only three defeats, yielding an average of half a goal per game and posting 20 shutouts. Phillips said she regretted there were so few goals for women to aspire to beyond local or provincial competition. She admitted she wanted to try her skills in professional or Olympic hockey and feared her career might be over before either or both of those opportunities came to pass.

The Shoppers Drug Mart tournament provided an opportunity to update developments in other provinces. The North Vancouver team brought a winning tradition: four consecutive provincial titles and the first gold medal awarded for women's hockey at the B.C. Winter Games. The North Vancouver Dynamos compiled a league record of 70–2–4 over the previous four years.

The Saskies, Saskatchewan's provincial champions, were a rejuvenation of a former Saskatchewan team — the Melfort Missilettes, a club that dominated women's hockey in the province until it disbanded in 1979. During the season, the Saskatchewan Ladies Hockey League and the Prince Albert Girls Hockey League were established. Major tournaments included the North Battleford Sweetheart Tournament and the University of Saskatchewan Tournament.

One-Armed Player in Major Women's Tournament

When the 19th annual Dominion Ladies Hockey Tournament was held in Mississauga in 1986, one of the players on a U.S. entry played despite a handicap. Patty Koch, 19, of Bridgeport, New York, was born without a right arm.

"The first time other players meet up with me on the ice, they kinda shy away from me," Koch said, laughing. "Then when they see I play the game just like they do, they come right after me."

Koch played for a team from New York State called the Southern Belles, and although her team lost both its tournament games, she stood out for her aggressive play. She has discovered that by using a longer stick and tucking it under her right shoulder she is able to handle the puck and shoot it reasonably hard.

"I can't get off a good slap shot," she admits. "But my wrist shot is pretty good. I get lots of practice playing against my brothers."

There was only one registered women's league in Manitoba in 1982–83. The Canadian Polish Athletic Club team posted a record of 29 wins and a tie during the 30-game schedule. Goals for exceeded goals against by 259 to 19.

The Ontario Women's Hockey Association announced a membership of 150 teams, ranging from atom to senior. The organization had certified 200 Level I and 80 Level II female coaches as well as 70 Level I and 20 Level II referees.

The Quebec situation had improved dramatically. Thirteen teams in three leagues were in operation and many other teams were clamouring for games. The first provincial championships in Quebec saw Concordia University, the Titans from the Montreal Hockey League, and the Belvederes from the Yamaska League battling for top honours. The eventual winners were the Titans, with a 15-year history of excellence on ice. A Quebec City representative reminded everyone that McGill had had a women's team as early as 1894, and in 1900 there was a five-team league comprising Westmount, the Victorias, Montreal, Quebec City, and Trois-Rivières.

Registered female teams in New Brunswick climbed from seven to 30 teams in one year, with the Saint John Women's Hockey League recognized as the most active and the circuit providing the highest calibre of play. Nova Scotia reported a decline in registered teams, although Sydney and Halifax were still hockey hotbeds. A major problem was the 10-hour round trip drive between the cities. The East Bay Ladies team obviously appealed to players whose surnames began with *M*. On the roster were the names MacDonald, MacNeill, McNeill, Mackinnon, MacArthur, McPhee, and MacPhil.

Prince Edward Island, the first province to register female players with a CAHA branch (in 1977), announced that all girls under 18 years of age playing in minor hockey associations were registered members of the Prince Edward Island Amateur Hockey Association and that the majority of teams were participating within the Northumberland, Bedeque, Central Queen's, and Alberton minor hockey associations.

In Newfoundland, where the St. John's Ladies Hockey League was organized in 1972, officials anticipated a doubling in size of the circuit for the 1983–84 season. Although a number of teams were playing in communities throughout the province, the primary area of interest was in St. John's.

THE MAJOR TURNING POINT for women's hockey came in 1987 when the first Women's World Hockey Tournament was held at Centennial Arena in North York, Ontario, and in Mississauga. The event was an overwhelming success, with teams representing Canada, Ontario, the United States, Sweden, Switzerland, Holland, and Japan competing against one another. Five other countries — Australia, China, Norway, the United Kingdom, and West Germany — sent delegates to watch and plan for the future, while reporters from *Sports Illustrated* and the *New York Times* covered the action. The tourney spawned other major championships in Europe and Asia and led to even larger World Championships. It was because of this event that the International Ice Hockey Federation decided that female hockey must become more prominent in the world of hockey.

Fran Rider, president of the host organization, the Ontario Women's Hockey Association, and chairperson of the world tournament, called it "a great step forward for women's hockey in our quest for future Olympic competition." She added: "The objective is to bring players from around the world together to compete and meet each other, to exhibit sportsmanship, and to have a good time. And it will give the public a chance to see girls play hockey at high skill levels."

Honorary chairperson Hazel McCallion showed up for the ceremonial opening face-off wearing her CCM Tacks and her chain of office. After the official drop of the puck, she took a whirl around the ice with a puck and stick. There were gasps when she tripped over the red carpet at centre ice and fell heavily to the ice. After a few moments, she got up, and to the delight of the crowd, skated in on goal and put the puck in the net.

The McCallion World Cup is a whopper of an award — one of the largest hockey trophies in existence. It is rivalled in height only by the Stanley Cup and weighs about 35 pounds. One of the players — a bartender perhaps — estimated the bowl would accommodate about 15 bottles of champagne.

Team Canada, represented by the Hamilton Golden Hawks and bolstered by players from Alberta and Saskatchewan, was financially strapped entering the tournament. Winners of the Canadian title at Moncton a month earlier, there was no money left in the kitty — not even for

Abby Hoffman Cup Winners

Year	Winner	Host City
1982	Agincourt Canadians (Ontario)	Brantford, Ontario
1983	Burlington Ladies (Ontario)	Brantford, Ontario
1984	Edmonton Chimos (Alberta)	Spruce Grove, Alberta
1985	Edmonton Chimos (Alberta)	Summerside, P.E.I.
1986	Hamilton Hawks (Ontario)	North Battleford, Saskatchewan
1987	Hamilton Hawks (Ontario)	Riverview, New Brunswick
1988	Sherbrooke (Quebec)	Burlington, Ontario
1989	Christin Automobiles (Quebec)	Coquitlam, B.C.
1990	Sherbrooke (Quebec)	Lloydminster, Saskatchewan
1991	Toronto Aeros (Ontario)	Verdun, Quebec
1992	Edmonton Chimos (Alberta)	Edmonton, Alberta
1993	Toronto Aeros (Ontario)	Ottawa, Ontario
1994	Selects (Quebec)	Winnipeg, Manitoba

practice time. An appeal for funds fell on deaf ears, except at the Dofasco plant in Hamilton where goalie Cathy Phillips was an employee. They donated their soft drink fund — $120 — and the team was able to pay for a couple of hours of ice time.

The Soviets were invited and the response was: "Sorry, we are unable to attend as there is no women's hockey in our country."

"Ha!" a Canadian sportswriter scoffed. "Given the comrades' love of the world stage, you can imagine a commissar of women's hockey was appointed to prepare for future championships the moment the invitation arrived."

Line Danielson, a 25-year-old centre with the Swedish club, said, "I wouldn't be surprised if they're building a team already." Danielson said European teams were handicapped because of uneven competition at home and too few games. "We played 17 games coming into this tournament. The Hamilton team has played 40." The Swedish team — Nacka HK — wouldn't have been able to compete in the tournament had it not been for NHL star defenceman Borje Salming, then a player for the Detroit Red Wings. Salming quietly donated $1,000 to sponsor the team. Nacka HK entered the tournament with an unbeaten streak of 65 games against Swedish opposition.

Karen Hebert, 25, a member of the Mississauga Warriors representing Ontario, was the luckiest competitor involved. Earlier, while vacationing in Florida, she wrote in the hotel guest book: "I'll be back as soon as I win the lottery back home." She returned home, bought a ticket, and won $1.6 million in Lotto 6/49. Then she kept her promise and went back to Florida.

Jackie Haggerty of the U.S. team felt so strongly about playing in the tournament that she quit her job as a tractor-trailer driver to come. And she paid her own way.

One game in the tournament, a thrilling clash between Canada and the United States, was thought by some to be the finest female hockey game ever played. One reporter called it "the best amateur hockey game I've ever seen." Canada won 2–1.

Fran Rider (centre), executive director of the Ontario Women's Hockey Association, with Team Canada 1992 gold medallists Karen Nystrom (left) and Angela James.
(Jane Sherk)

Team Canada swept to the championship and the McCallion Cup with a 4–0 victory over Ontario (Mississauga Warriors) in the title game. Colleen Kohen, who scored Canada's second goal, said the tournament was the experience of a lifetime. "It's a highlight I'll never forget. The friendships I've made have been great."

Mississauga high school teacher Marion Coveny was the captain of Team Canada. After 17 years of playing with little recognition, Coveny, 32, said: "This is a dream come true — women's hockey making the big time. Every time I watch the NHL I envy those players. Women just don't get that kind of opportunity." When Coveny stepped onto the ice for her first tournament game, she turned and looked around, not realizing *Toronto Star* reporter

Top Defender Advocates Bodychecking

In 1986 Joey Bush, a veteran of 19 consecutive Dominion Ladies tournaments, decided to bow out of hockey. Two years earlier Bush had been diagnosed with multiple sclerosis. At 35 the Scarborough star had accumulated more than 40 trophies, including one for being the most valuable defender in the 1984 nationals in Edmonton. She also refereed for 20 years.

"I got started as a 10-year-old at the Don Mills Arena," she told Lois Kalchman of the Toronto Star. "I pestered the late Harry Lazerenko to let me play, and he finally did. Harry taught me self-discipline on the ice. He was able to bring out whatever talent I had. Back then we played outdoors a lot and didn't wear any equipment. Later, when we put shinpads on (right over our pants) and then slipped into regular hockey pants, why we felt like monsters!"

While never a rough player, Bush voiced strong opinions on bodychecking and other issues in women's hockey. "I am dead set against interlocking males and females on the same teams," she said. "And I believe that bodychecking is a part of the game. To learn how to give a hit or take a hit or to slip away from a checker is a skill all players must learn. It's really quite an art."

Lois Kalchman was standing nearby. Coveny murmured, "One giant step for womankind," and Kalchman scribbled the comment in her notebook.

At one of the press receptions Kalchman was in line at the buffet when a member of the Swedish team nudged her from behind. "Tell me, please, what kind of strange dish is that?" the visitor asked. "Why, it's Swedish meatballs, dear," Kalchman replied, and everyone laughed.

Winning coach Dave McMaster commented, "The whole atmosphere of the tournament was positive and hopefully we'll have the Olympics next."

The United States downed Sweden 5–0 to pick up the bronze medal, while Switzerland blanked Japan 4–0 for fifth position. Canada dominated the awards ceremony as Edmonton native Dawn McGuire was named MVP and Cathy Phillips was named top goaltender.

After the initial national tournament in 1982, the following letter by Aniko Varpalotai appeared in the *Globe and Mail:*

Female Player Convicted of Assault

On June 22, 1988, a Windsor area woman became the first hockey player to be convicted of assaulting an official during a game. In 1986 nurse Trudy Banwell, then 24, was playing for a women's team from Harrow, Ontario, in the provincial championships at Mississauga when she slammed referee Angela James to the ice. Then she assaulted linesman Barb Jeffrey, separating her shoulder.

Convicted of two counts of assault, Banwell was given a conditional discharge and two years' probation and ordered her to serve 200 hours of community work. The Ontario Women's Hockey Association handed Banwell a lifetime suspension. Bev Gaidosch, director of female hockey for the CAHA, said she believed it was the first time in Canada a female hockey player had been convicted on criminal charges.

I was disappointed once more in the newspaper that purports to be Canada's "national" newspaper for its lack of coverage of the first World Women's Ice Hockey Tournament, held at the North York Centennial Arena. Not only does the *Globe and Mail* persist in perpetuating the notion that only men play sports, particularly hockey (thus neglecting half the nation, at least), but it is denying to its readership information about an international historic event.

Surely in the midst of NHL trivia readers would welcome a change of pace — and the women who worked so hard to make this world-class event possible deserve our praise and recognition.

West Germany's Wolfgang Sorge said the next world event would be back in Ontario in 1989. "I will report what I have seen here to Dr. Sabetzki [president of the IIHF]," Sorge said. "I am sure he will support women's hockey. Two years hence it might be [an IIHF] World Championship — the first one ever."

In 1990 in Quebec a committee appointed by the provincial government recommended greater opportunities for women players, including a provincial tournament for the 50 existing women's teams in the province. The committee, which included former Montreal Canadiens star Jacques Lemaire, recommended that young girls be allowed to compete on an equal basis on boys' teams until age 13.

Thanks to the support of federal, provincial, and municipal politicians, women's hockey made huge gains in the eighties. National Championships had been held since 1982 and a female council had become an important voice within the Canadian Amateur Hockey Association. Furthermore, groundwork laid by the Ontario Women's Hockey Association and others in the decade led to the successful integration of female hockey into the 1991 Canada Games. The 1990s would bring even more delightful surprises: registrations in record numbers, women invading men's professional hockey, bona fide World Championships and, best of all, acceptance into the Olympic Games.

7

An Olympic Goal

THE NINETIES

Team Canada wins gold again, this time in Tampere, Finland, in 1992. For these women no Stanley Cup victory could be sweeter.

(Jane Sherk)

IN MARCH 1990 an enthusiastic crowd of almost 9,000, many of them waving pink-and-white Canadian flags in recognition of the Canadian team's flashy pink-and-white uniforms, cheered Canada on to a 5–2 victory over the United States in the deciding game of the inaugural IIHF-sanctioned Women's World Championship in Ottawa. After the historic victory, Canadian team captain Sue Scherer, dodging a spray of champagne in the dressing room, said, "Now we're on top of the world. It's been a great week for women's hockey."

Indeed it had been. Until the 1990 tournament in Ottawa, most of the players involved were more accustomed to playing before sparse crowds, largely friends and family, rather than a flag-waving mob like the one in the Ottawa Civic Centre and the untold thousands watching on television.

Some of the players from overseas appeared to be overwhelmed by the event. In Sweden only about 600 females played hockey. A Japanese player talked of only 30 or 40 teams in her country. The Canadian women overcame many obstacles to become members of their national team. They had known the frustration of competing for ice time with male teams and figure skaters. Many had been turned down in their quest for sponsors and told that women's hockey was not very popular from a marketing standpoint.

Still, their numbers kept growing. It was estimated that 7,500 women were playing in CAHA leagues across Canada. Another 18,000 were said to be playing high school, university, or recreational hockey. According to D'arcy Jenish, writing in *Maclean's*, there were 4,600 CAHA players and 327 teams in Ontario. Alberta was a distant second with 940 players and 57 teams.

All week the Canadian uniforms underwent much scrutiny. Jane O'Hara, writing in the *Ottawa Sun*, called them "the wussiest uniforms you've ever seen." They were designed by Tackla, a Finnish sportswear company, which paid the International Ice Hockey Federation $250,000 for the rights to outfit all of the competing teams. O'Hara was not a fan of pink. "Real women don't wear pink," she wrote. "Pink does not inspire fear. Pink does not spark aggression. When you think about battling it out in the corners, you do not think pink. As a team colour, pink stinks." Others disagreed, including many of the players, who said the uniform colours were "cool" and "different . . . but not the least bit outrageous."

The Canadian women breezed through the nonmedal round, outshooting their opponents 176–23 and outscoring them 50–1. The tiny Japanese fell 18–0 and were outshot 57–8.

In the title game with the United States, Canada fell behind early and trailed 2–0 after the first period. But coach Dave McMaster wasn't concerned. "This team has too much character and too much talent to be down for long. I knew we'd start to score." He was right. Canada bounced back with five straight goals to win 5–2. France St. Louis led the attack with two goals and two assists, while Geraldine Heaney, Susana Yuen, and Judy Diduck added singles. Heaney's goal was spectacular. She broke in from the blue line, vaulted past a defender and, while falling, fired a shot over the shoulder of U.S. goalie Kelly Dyer. Finland, which lost to both Canada and the United States earlier in the week, settled for the bronze medal, beating Sweden 6–3 in a consolation game.

Sports Illustrated was on hand for the tournament, and correspondent Paul Fichtenbaum wrote:

> Women's hockey is not the pajama party you might imagine. In the mid-1970s, when many U.S. college programs started, some women arrived for tryouts in figure skates with pom-poms on them or even carried their equipment in pillow cases embroidered with ballerinas. Now they know how to play the game. Their breakout plays are the same ones used in the NHL, their passes are short and crisp, their skating strong and their puckhandling skills extraordinary.

The fans saw women crunching one another in the corners and in the slot. Under the tournament rules bodychecking was legal. It was an issue that had created much controversy. Ironically it was the Europeans who supported full-body checking, while the Canadians, known for their physical play, led those opposed to it. Pat Reid, the tournament's manager, said Canadian officials felt the women's game would develop more rapidly if the speed and individual skills were promoted and the rough play deemphasized.

With bodychecking allowed the hard hitting did a lot of damage, but the competitors took their bruises in stride. Canada's France St. Louis spent three days in hospital after being slashed across the throat, but she was released in time to collect four points in the championship game. What delighted the fans was not the physical play but the high level of skills displayed and the outstanding teamwork that became a tournament feature.

Canadian defender Dawn McGuire of Burlington was named the tournament's most valuable defender and an all-star. She was voted MVP of the title game.

U.S. coach Don McLeod tried to motivate his players with a message from President George Bush, who said he was rooting for another "Miracle on Ice" (referring to the U.S.

Olympic team's 1980 hockey triumph at Lake Placid). McLeod said it came down to his team being unable to sustain an emotional high against a more talented opponent. "Canada was simply better than us. That's all there was to it," he told reporters.

TSN's coverage of the week-long event was credited with triggering a boom in players signing up for hockey at the grass-roots level. "The TV coverage showed the viewers that women's hockey was a very exciting game," Canadian goaltender Cathy Phillips said. "Parents could see that their daughters could play hockey at a high level, and it was no disgrace to be a female player. It's hard to sell fathers in getting their daughters involved, but thanks to television that is all changing."

A remarkable 12-year-old, Samantha Holmes journeyed from her Mississauga home to Ottawa for the big event and later sent me a report on her trip to Ottawa:

It was the first World Hockey Championships and I wanted to be part of history. From the time of my arrival in Ottawa I saw hockey people. I was really treated special and that made me feel good.

One of the first people I met was head coach Dave McMaster. His first words were, "Sam, what kept you? I thought you'd be here a week ago. Our team needs your support."

The next person I met was Mabel Boyd. She is known as the grandmother of female hockey. She had just arrived and she was happy to see someone from Mississauga. She asked me if I had my hockey equipment and when I answered "Yes," she said, "I do, too. Let's show the folks here in Ottawa how to play the game." Mabel is 68 and has been playing hockey for over fifty years. Also she started the Mississauga Hockey League, so if it wasn't for Mabel I wouldn't be playing.

Meeting the players was the highlight of my trip. All the players and coaching staff were awesome to me. They would take me into the dressing room and they always had a souvenir for me. Don McLeod, the coach of the U.S. team, asked me if I was 17 yet. When I told him I was only 12, he said it seemed like I'd been around as long as him.

My favourite players and closest friends were Angela James, Margot Verlaan and Theresa Hutchinson. I made close friends with many others from across Canada. France Montour from Quebec could not speak English, but the night the team won the gold she put her medal around my neck and said, "Yours." I refused it politely and said, "Thank you but I can't accept. I will earn my own someday."

There were less than four thousand fans on hand at the Civic Centre for this great moment, but millions more watched on TV as it was sent by satellite to many countries in the world. The excitement mounted as Abigail Hoffman dropped the puck. Canada was the favourite, and it was easy to see why from the moment they stepped on the ice.

Team Sweden were considered competitive but not strong. The first goal came at the ten minute mark as my friend and hockey hero for six years scored the first goal of the championships. Angela James was known as the Wayne Gretzky of female hockey, and she lived up to that name in no time. The puck from that goal will go in the Hockey Hall of Fame and A.J., who has given so much support to my hockey dreams, goes down in history. The moment couldn't have been any more exciting than if my own time had arrived. Later, in a TV interview, Angela said, "We're doing this for the little girls who are coming up," and somehow I felt she was talking to me personally.

The first game was pretty one-sided with Team Canada defeating Sweden by 15–1. Angela James ended up getting a hat trick, but something else happened just as important — the world saw that girls can play hockey, too.

Canada met the U.S. in the championship game. Maybe I didn't mention it but Team Canada's sweaters were hot pink. The scene in Ottawa by the final game was one of pink madness. Restaurants and hotels offered "pink specials" in the form of pink drinks. Most spectators wore pink. The ushers at Lansdowne Park wore pink bow ties and pink carnations. It was like a wedding between male and female hockey, as many hockey fans decked their cars in pink pom-poms. The Canadian players wore pink ribbons in their hair.

The scene was set for a Team Canada victory and that's exactly what happened. The U.S. players were big and strong — an excellent team. They had younger players who frustrated easily and they spent a lot of time in the penalty box. Team Canada was confident and experienced. They played wisely and like a team, and walked away victorious. The games went down in history and women's hockey is here to stay.

The Ottawa tournament had a tremendous impact on women's hockey everywhere, including the marketplace. According to the Canadian Amateur Hockey Association, the number of registered females playing the game in Canada jumped 75 percent in one year, with Ontario accounting for more than half that surge. Close to 9,000 females were playing on 352 teams in the Ontario Women's Hockey Association.

The boom also led to a number of hockey schools for female players. Stephanie Boyd had 36 girls attend her first hockey school in Gravenhurst, Ontario. Her second-year enrollment soared to 85. High school teacher Margot Page conducted a summer clinic at the University of Waterloo. She told the *Toronto Star*'s Mary Ormsby: "I love looking at the intent faces that are so eager to learn everything they can about hockey. And if some of these players go on to play in the World Championships or the Olympics one day, I'll have played a small role in their success. That would make me feel really good."

**Dedicated hockey player
Samantha Holmes at age 15.**

(Marilyn Holmes Collection)

Many world-class players were recruited to teach their skills in other countries. The Japanese hired a small group of Canada's elite players to instruct their young players and coaches.

One year after the Ottawa tournament, game one of which I enjoyed from rinkside handling the microphone for the pregame ceremonies, I was invited to participate in a special exhibition game at the Hamilton Mountain Arena. There I suited up with former NHL stars Ken Dryden, Jim McKenny, and Darryl Sittler, along with CFL stars Rocky DiPietro, Wally Zatylny, and Mike Kerrigan. We were opposed by members of the 1990 Team Canada women's squad, their lineup bolstered by Mississauga's ageless mayor, Hazel McCallion, and a pair of future stars, Meaghan Sittler and Sarah Dryden. The referee was former NHL arbiter Bill Friday

The game was in honour of one of women's hockey's greatest goalies — Cathy Phillips. After backstopping Canada to the gold medal in Ottawa a few months earlier, Phillips was diagnosed with a benign brain tumour. Surgery was successful, and Cathy was in the midst of a remarkable comeback.

Phillips had achieved more goals in her life than most athletes hope to attain in a lifetime. She was universally recognized as the top female goalie in women's hockey. During 17 years of play for Burlington and Hamilton teams, she had been voted "top goalie" 14 times. Twice she was voted MVP of her Senior A league. She participated in seven of the nine Canadian Women's National Championship finals, winning four gold medals, two silver, and a bronze.

Veteran goaltender Cathy Phillips drops the puck at a special exhibition game in her honour on January 26, 1991, in Hamilton, Ontario. The 1990 Team Canada gold medallists took on former NHL stars. In uniform on the left are Ken Dryden and Darryl Sittler; on the right, Meaghan Sittler and Sarah Dryden.

(Ontario Women's Hockey Association)

In 1987 she was named most valuable goalie of the first Women's World Tournament held in Mississauga and North York.

A few days before the Hamilton game Phillips met her goaltending hero — Russian superstar Vladislav Tretiak, who made a surprise stopover in Mississauga while on his way to an engagement in Calgary.

"All goalies should support each other through good times and bad," Tretiak said. "Goalies are special people and they have a special understanding of each other." He presented Phillips with an autographed copy of his autobiography.

In April 1992 at a press conference at Maple Leaf Gardens prior to departing for Tampere, Finland, and the second IIHF-sanctioned World Championship, Team Canada star Sue Scherer told the media: "I speak from an older player's perspective. I don't use the word veteran because wherever we go and whatever we do hockey presents us with rookie experiences. This team is tremendously talented. From 1990 to '92 the calibre of talent on this team has jumped fourfold. The average age has dropped except for yours truly. Somehow my age keeps going up. Still, for someone who has played for 25 years I find I never stop learning. This second World Championship will offer us a chance to present hockey to the world in a fashion that is exciting and entertaining. Hopefully it will bring the women's game to the forefront once again.

"Hopes and dreams? You never lose your hopes and dreams. I've never lost my passion for hockey, the joy that comes from playing, the peculiar feeling that comes from a little bubble inside me somewhere. Every time I put on my skates — from the age of three until now — there's this little bubble inside me that says I've got to play! I've got to play hockey! It's the same feeling every player on this team knows and shares. The chemistry is unbelievable, the talent is incredible. Believe me, we will represent Canada in a manner that will make everyone proud."

I was intrigued with Sue Scherer's comments about the "little bubble inside" and asked her if she would expand on the subject. She laughed and said: "It's a little bubble that I noticed when my parents first took me skating. And I felt it again when I first played street hockey with my brothers. It's simply a feeling of excitement about this game that catches hold of you and simply won't go away. Perhaps it comes from growing up in a hockey-playing family [with six brothers], but it's not just in me. I know it exists in a lot of people who love this game, people whose hearts and souls are into it. I don't think I'll ever lose it. After all this time I don't think I could. It's something that motivates you and puts a smile on your face the moment you put your skates on. It's there when you take a stick in your hands and put a helmet on your head.

Sometimes you don't care if you've got another stitch of equipment on or who's skating on the ice with you. It's just a feeling of exhilaration, the thrill of being a player in the game."

In April 1992 Canada won its second successive IIHF world hockey title in Tampere, Finland, by thrashing the United States 8–0 in the title game. Nancy Drolet and Danielle Goyette, two stars from Quebec, went on a scoring rampage against the Americans. Drolet, of Drummondville, scored three goals and Goyette, of Ste-Foy, near Quebec City, added a goal and three assists in the gold medal game. Drolet said: "It was the best moment of my career." A teammate of Manon Rhéaume for three years and a close friend, Drolet said all the atten-

Nancy Drolet (left), Cassie Campbell, and Danielle Goyette at training camp for the 1994 World Championship in Lake Placid.
(Jane Sherk)

tion Rhéaume received for playing pro hockey with men provided badly needed publicity for women's hockey. "The point is not to compare women's hockey with men's," she insisted. "People have to see and appreciate women's hockey on its own."

Head coach Rick Polutnik talked of his players' response to coaching: "Their thirst for knowledge is great and their commitment to a team concept makes it easy to coach them in a short-term competition. All in all, it was a great experience. I have a set of memories I'll treasure forever."

It was obvious in Finland that confusion still existed over the definition of bodychecking in women's hockey. Some of the European nations wanted it reintroduced, stating that women's hockey should be exactly the same as the men's. Others questioned the Canadian definition of a bodycheck, recalling some of the hard hits that rattled competitors in the 1990 tournament in Ottawa.

Back in Canada, after the tournament, team members Sue Scherer and Heather Ginzel appeared on television on *The Dini Petty Show*. They pointed out that the medals they had won in Finland had pictures of men on them. "They should have had depictions of women on the medals," the players rightly complained. They also told Petty, "When we play in these tournaments, we compete as Canadians — not English or French Canadians."

Canada's domination in Finland wasn't a fair indicator of the progress other nations had made, according to Glynis Peters, manager of the CAHA's female hockey council. Peters was impressed with the strides made by the Chinese. "It was really interesting to see how good they were," she said. "They were really aggressive and a lot better skaters than we expected. It was really heartwarming to see that China was offering us very good hockey."

The gold medal triumph, unlike previous women's tournaments that went virtually unnoticed by the media, made the front pages of newspapers coast-to-coast and was the lead story on most radio and television broadcasts.

A few months later, on November 17, 1992, women players around the world rejoiced when the International Olympic Committee announced that their game would be part of the 1998 Olympic Games in Nagano, Japan. In Ottawa Glynis Peters said it was "touch and go" until the decision was reached.

"There was a lot of resistance to women's hockey in Japan," she told Mary Ormsby of the *Toronto Star.* "The organizers didn't want to pay for hosting another sport and, besides that, the Japanese don't have a strong women's hockey program. Now they'll have to finance an entirely new sports operation to bring their team up to Olympic standards in a few years. They were really reluctant to commit to that." With the help of Gordon Renwick of the IIHF, the CAHA organized a program, including coaching exchanges, to assist the Japanese in raising the level of play in Japan.

Ontario Women's Hockey Association president Fran Rider said: "Women's hockey in the Olympics will have a major impact on the entire sport throughout the world. It will bring out the young players and will open the doors for the kind of government and corporate support that has not been there for non-Olympic sports. Young players can now see the light at the end of the tunnel . . . something they could never see before."

Greater publicity and attention than ever before was focused on the national team in 1994 when it prepared to defend the world title at Lake Placid, New York. The event was scheduled for the same arena where the U.S. men's Olympic team created a "Miracle on Ice" in 1980. "There's no doubt the U.S. women will be using that as a motivational tool," said Canadian coach Les Lawton, head coach at Montreal's Concordia University.

Lawton and his assistant coaches, Shannon Miller, a Calgary police officer, and Melody Davidson, recreation director for the town of Castor, Alberta, selected an impressive mix of newcomers and veterans from a January tryout camp. Only six members of the 1990 and 1992 championship teams remained — 35-year-old France St. Louis of Montreal, Angela James of

Thornhill, Geraldine Heaney of Toronto, Judy Diduck of Vancouver, Margot Verlaan Page (married since 1992) of Kitchener, and Stacy Wilson of New Brunswick.

A newcomer who won much praise was Calgary's Hayley Wickenheiser, 15, a distant cousin of former NHL star Doug Wickenheiser. "Hayley may be the youngest player in the forthcoming tournament," coach Lawton said, "but she has the maturity of a 20-year-old. And she has all the skills of a veteran."

"I don't think the coaching staff had any choice but to select Hayley," 29-year-old Angela James said. "She's that good. And it's good for women's hockey to see such talented young players emerging." Wickenheiser said she jumped "six feet in the air" when Lawton told her she was going to Lake Placid.

Manon Rhéaume, who provided the national team with outstanding netminding in 1992 and who was one of only three professional female goaltenders on the planet, joined the team from the Nashville Knights of the East Coast Hockey League for another crack at international play. With Nashville she had a record of five wins and a tie in six starts. But she wouldn't be the only pro in the competition. Sharing the goaltending duties for the U.S. squad were Erin Whitten and Kelly Dyer, both of whom were rookies in minor pro hockey. Early in the 1993–94 season Whitten became the first woman to record a win in pro hockey. Dyer was on the roster of the West Palm Beach Blaze of the Florida Sunshine League.

Canada lost an exhibition game to Finland 6–3 — an indication that the Finns were a serious threat to dislodge Canada from their roost at Lake Placid — and edged the stubborn Americans 3–2 in a second pre-tournament encounter. But when real play got under way, Les Lawton's Canadians were invincible. On Sunday afternoon, April 17,

1990 IIHF Women's World Championship Results

Ottawa, Canada
March 19–25, 1990

Final Ranking and Overall Records

No.	Team	GP	W	L	T	GF	GA
1.	Canada	5	5	0	0	61	8
2.	USA	5	4	1	0	50	15
3.	Finland	5	3	2	0	35	15
4.	Sweden	5	2	3	0	25	35
5.	Switzerland	5	3	2	0	23	39
6.	Norway	5	1	4	0	16	45
7.	Germany	5	2	3	0	16	33
8.	Japan	5	0	5	0	11	47

Scoring Leaders

No.	Name	Team	GP	G	A	TP	PIM
1.	Cindy Curley	USA	5	11	12	23	2
2.	Tina Cardinale	USA	5	5	10	15	2
3.	Cammi Granato	USA	5	9	5	14	4
4.	Kim Urech	SUI	5	8	6	14	2
5.	Angela James	CAN	5	11	2	13	10

Goaltending Leaders

No.	Name	Team	GPI	Mins.	GA	SPG	SVS%	GAA
1.	Cathy Phillips	CAN	4	156.0	3	32	.906	1.15
2.	Denise Caron	CAN	3	144.0	5	32	.844	2.08
3.	Aurelia Vonderstrab	GER	3	180.0	10	65	.846	3.33
4.	Kelly Dyer	USA	4	200.0	12	83	.855	3.60
5.	Liisa-Maria Sneck	FIN	4	240.0	15	89	.832	3.75

1992 IIHF Women's World Championship Results

Tampere, Finland
April 20–26, 1992

Final Ranking and Overall Records

No.	Team	GP	W	L	T	GF	GA
1.	Canada	5	5	0	0	38	3
2.	USA	5	4	1	0	37	16
3.	Finland	5	3	2	0	32	17
4.	Sweden	5	2	3	0	19	20
5.	China	5	3	2	0	11	18
6.	Norway	5	2	3	0	9	21
7.	Denmark	5	1	4	0	7	24
8.	Switzerland	5	0	5	0	6	40

Scoring Leaders

No.	Name	Team	GP	G	A	TP	PIM
1.	Cammi Granato	USA	5	8	2	10	2
2.	Danielle Goyette	CAN	5	3	7	10	2
3.	Andria Hunter	CAN	5	5	4	9	0
4.	Lisa Brown	USA	5	2	7	9	8
5.	Shelley Looney	USA	5	1	8	9	2

Goaltending Leaders

No.	Name	Team	GPI	Mins.	GA	SPG	SVS%	GAA
1.	Marie-Claude Roy	CAN	2	120.0	1	24	.958	0.50
2.	Manon Rhéaume	CAN	3	180.0	2	45	.957	0.67
3.	Katariina Ahonen	FIN	3	149.4	5	42	.881	2.01
4.	Annica Ahlén	SWE	3	190.0	8	95	.916	2.53
5.	Hong Guo	PRC	5	310.0	18	141	.872	3.48
6.	Erin Whitten	USA	4	228.4	14	94	.851	3.68

1994 IIHF Women's World Championship Results

Lake Placid, New York, U.S.A.
April 11–17, 1994

Final Ranking and Overall Records

No.	Team	GP	W	L	T	GF	GA
1.	Canada	5	5	0	0	37	7
2.	USA	5	4	1	0	41	10
3.	Finland	5	3	2	0	40	8
4.	China	5	1	3	1	17	34
5.	Sweden	5	3	1	1	22	17
6.	Norway	5	1	4	0	12	33
7.	Switzerland	5	1	4	0	10	30
8.	Germany	5	0	5	0	6	46

Scoring Leaders

No.	Name	Team	GP	G	A	TP	PIM
1.	Riikka Nieminen	FIN	5	4	9	13	4
2.	Danielle Goyette	CAN	5	9	3	12	0
3.	Karyn Bye	USA	5	6	6	12	2
4.	Cammi Granato	USA	5	5	7	12	6
5.	Hongmei Liu	PRC	5	8	3	11	2
6.	Tiia Reima	FIN	5	7	4	11	6

Goaltending Leaders

No.	Name	Team	GPI	Mins.	GA	SPG	SVS%	GAA
1.	Kati Ahonen	FIN	2	80.0	1	20	.950	0.75
2.	Lesley Reddon	CAN	2	91.0	1	15	.933	0.66
3.	Liisa-Maria Sneck	FIN	4	220.0	7	85	.917	1.91
4.	Kelly Dyer	USA	2	120.0	3	24	.875	1.50
5.	Manon Rhéaume	CAN	4	209.0	6	44	.863	1.72

they met the U.S. women for the third straight time in a World Championship match-up. Earlier, in a battle for bronze, Finland had defeated China 8–1.

After falling behind 1–0 in the first period, Canada's Angela James and Danielle Goyette led a red-shirted charge with two goals each. Stacy Wilson and France St. Louis added singles, and Canada emerged with a 6–3 victory over the United States. James was named MVP of the final game but shrugged off the personal recognition. "There's only one MVP," she said, "but there are 20 gold medals and that's what is important."

U.S. coach Karen Kay had prepared her team well. It helped when Mike Eruzione, who scored the winning goal for the U.S. against the Soviet powerhouse in 1980, phoned to deliver an inspirational pregame message that included advice to stay out of the penalty box. Star player Cammi Granato had received good-luck telegrams from her brother Tony and members of the Los Angeles Kings. Tony had even sent along a pair of lucky wristbands — a gift from Wayne Gretzky — and Cammi promised to wear them with pride.

Some of Gretzky's magic must have been in the wristbands, for Granato played a superb game, but the message from Eruzione fell on deaf ears. A series of penalties crippled the Americans, and Canada took advantage, rapping in three power-play goals.

The firm in charge of promoting the event made one glaring faux pas. On the cover of the official program two male hockey players were depicted.

Canada's three successive IIHF World Championships were equalled only once before by Canadian men's teams from 1951 to 1953. The Canadian women remained unbeaten after three trips to the worlds, with a glossy 15–0 mark. The U.S. record fell to 12–3. Both teams hope to reach the finals again in the 1996 world tournament slated for a Canadian site (yet to be selected) and two years later when women's hockey makes its debut at the Winter Olympics in Japan.

MANON RHÉAUME MADE HISTORY on November 26, 1991, when she became the first woman to play in a major Junior game. She skated on in relief of Trois-Rivières Draveurs netminder Jocelyn Thibeault midway through a game with Granby. The score was tied 5–5, and Rhéaume gave up three goals on 13 shots in 17 minutes of play. She was forced out of the game when a high slap shot off the stick of Philippe Boucher gashed her head.

After the game Rhéaume told reporters, "I was very nervous. If I went into a situation like that again, I wouldn't be so nervous. I will do much better in the future."

Many didn't think so. In six games that same season with Louiseville of the Quebec Tier II Hockey League she had a goals-against average of 8.88 and failed to win even one game for the last-place Louiseville club. But her coach in Louiseville supported her. Yves Beaudry said: "Manon was tough, very tough. She was a good team member. She never backed down, but she had a tough time because the opposing players drove to the net very hard."

Manon said: "When I played in Junior, the team that played against me . . . well, the coach told them to shoot very high to make me afraid. But I'm not afraid. Sometimes it can be very dangerous if all the shots are high to the head. Two or three is okay, but if all the shots are at my head, well . . . it's not good, but still I'm not afraid. I like to face very fast shots. There is a difference between boys' shots and girls' shots. The boys are much faster."

Manon Rhéaume (right) with Team Canada '92 coach Pierre Charette.

When she played in the Junior A game, she knew people were interested in her and there would be demands on her time. But she was surprised at the extent of her notoriety. "I knew I was going to have some publicity, maybe even from Montreal," she recalled, "but I had many, many interviews from all over the United States and Europe. And Canada, of course. Many TV shows and many radios shows called from around the world. David Letterman wanted me on his show, but I was afraid for my English. I understand English pretty well, but sometimes there are words I don't understand or I get them mixed up. It was a difficult decision, but I didn't want to look foolish on TV. Maybe next time . . ."

Even *Playboy* took notice of the attractive netminder and offered her $75,000 to pose for a layout in the nude. Manon instantly refused. "They could have offered me a million and I still wouldn't do that," she said.

Manon began to skate when she was three years old. It was on a small rink her father built for her brothers to play on. "When we played outside as children, my brothers put me in goal and shot on me. My father coached my youngest brother, and in this team we had just players because we learned to skate before we had a goalie. One day my father wanted to make a tournament and we didn't have a goalie, so I said to my father, 'I would like to be goalie for this tournament.' He said all right and it started like this.

"It was fun, because the first day I came to play I dressed at home. When I arrived at the rink, I was wearing my helmet because my father didn't want the parents at the game to say, 'Oh, it's a girl in goal. That's not good.' But when they saw me play in goal, afterward they said, 'Oh, *he* was good.'

"You don't have to look like a boy to play with boys. You don't have to walk like a boy or talk like a boy to play with boys. It's very important to have the respect of all the players. When you're a girl and you show them you can play well, they accept you and they respect you more."

After Rhéaume helped the Canadian women's national team to a first-place finish in the 1992 world championships, she was invited to the training camp of the NHL's Tampa Bay Lightning. General manager Phil Esposito admitted that publicity was a factor in his decision to bring Rhéaume to camp. "Even so, she deserves a chance," Esposito still insisted.

Her big moment came in the preseason when she became the first woman to play in one of the four major sports. The 20-year-old played the first period of an NHL game between Tampa Bay and St. Louis. She faced nine shots and allowed two goals and drew a standing ovation from the fans in the Florida State Fairgrounds Expo Hall.

"For me it's a chance to play," she said before the game. "If I don't try, if I don't get the chance, then I don't know what I can do." To those who questioned her right to be part of an NHL training camp, she said, "I mean, I can skate. I can stop a puck. I haven't been an embarrassment."

After the game, Esposito said he had seen enough to offer her a contract with the minor league Atlanta Knights, Tampa's International Hockey League farm club. "We want her in our organization for a long, long time," Esposito said.

When asked if he thought she would be good enough to play in the NHL, he said, "She can if she progresses like we've seen. There are not many 20-year-olds — men or women — who can play goal in the NHL. She has God-given talent. You don't just stand in goal like that. You have to have talent to do that."

"They're actually going to pay me to play hockey," Rhéaume said, laughing. "I really can't believe it. All I did was come here hoping for a chance and hoping to improve. This is what all little boys dream about. I never dreamed it would happen to me."

Rhéaume signed a three-year pact with Tampa Bay, with provisions in her contract stipulating that she wouldn't be exploited. Her appearance in a Tampa Bay uniform brought requests from all the major talk shows, including a second bid from the Letterman show. Arsenio Hall quipped, "Who knows more about stopping boys from scoring than girls?"

On December 13, 1993, Rhéaume became the first female to play goal in a regular-season professional game when she took over from David Littman in a game against Salt Lake City. The Atlanta crowd went wild when Manon skated out to start the second period. They shrieked, "Ma-non, Ma-non!" as she took her place in goal. She stopped three shots, allowed a goal, and had a second goal nullified by an interference penalty. She played 5:49 before Littman returned. Salt Lake City won the contest 4–1.

For the 1993–94 season it was decided Rhéaume would benefit from playing in the East Coast Hockey League. She began with Nashville and was traded to Knoxville. If changing teams bothered her, she didn't let on. "If there's a rink, a place to pray, and a shopping mall, then I am happy," she told reporters.

At the end of the season she switched to women's hockey and played for Canada's national team in the World Championship at Lake Placid. She reported in the best shape of her life, having dropped 10 pounds while playing in the pro league.

At Lake Placid Mary Ormsby of the *Toronto Star* helped to dispel several myths about Rhéaume: that she was a selfish glory seeker, that her teammates hated her, and that she couldn't play hockey. Ormsby said all three were untrue and wrote:

Manon passionately loves the game. She continues to reap benefits that other players can only dream about. She sincerely believes that achievement as a group supersedes individual honors. Simply put, the game's most glamorous star is the ultimate team player.

When deluged with media requests, she tried to keep interviews short because she didn't want to hold up the team bus.

The day before the Canada–United States gold medal final, Rhéaume cancelled a photo shoot when the photographer asked her and U.S. counterpart [goalie] Erin Whitten to raise their fists against each other.

"I was so mad," [Rhéaume told Ormsby]. "I said this gold medal game is not about me and Erin. It's about Canada and the United States."

Rhéaume went out of her way to comfort a young teammate who had failed to score a goal in the tournament and was disconsolate. She told the teenager not to be concerned, that winning the gold medal as a team was all that counted, not who scored the goals or collected the shutouts.

In Lake Placid she earned the respect of her teammates, some of whom felt she had made the 1992 team, not on merit but because of her reputation and celebrity. Ormsby noted: "She is swarmed by autograph seekers in restaurants and seethes when she reads printed lies about her love life and her salary."

Rhéaume has a unique life in hockey, playing for a male pro team one minute, the women's national team the next. She has an autobiography on the market, lucrative endorsement opportunities, and a summer job playing goal for the New Jersey Rockin' Rollers of the Roller International League.

"I love my life because I can play hockey every day," she says.

EVER SINCE ABBY HOFFMAN played on a boys' team in the fifties there has been controversy over girls playing organized hockey with boys. The controversy was rekindled when Manon Rhéaume signed a professional contract with the Atlanta Knights of the International Hockey League in 1993.

When Angela James, one of the best female players in Canada, was asked about Manon Rhéaume joining a pro team, she said, "I think it's great. It's a start, right?" James, a forward, has been called the female version of Wayne Gretzky. Even though she has played all her life with women's teams, she has had the opportunity to practise with some top-level Junior A players and a few NHL stars. She is the first to admit that she is not strong enough to keep up with the men, nor does she want to.

"I think we have to keep the two games separate," she says. "You know, men's hockey is men's hockey and women's hockey is women's hockey. It's like the golf or the tennis tour. Women should be content to compete against each other. I think if we can continue to raise the level of women's play and play in the Olympics, then we'll be taken a little more seriously."

Fran Rider says all the attention on Manon Rhéaume is both good and bad for the sport. "We're in a catch-22 situation. If the top or even average female players go into a male program, it's going to dilute the female program. In cases like Manon's, we give her full credit for possessing a lot of talent. She really is an outstanding athlete who truly loves hockey. This does point out a weakness in our public relations efforts, though, because we've got players who have led the world since 1982 — Dawn McGuire, Cathy Phillips, Angela James, and France St. Louis, to name a few — and these are not household names. But because Manon is playing in a male program she has become a household name. The other women I mentioned should be just as famous."

France St. Louis fears for the future if young girls try to follow in the footsteps of Manon. "If all the girls go out and play with guys, there won't be any women's teams," she says. "I think we women should stick together. We have some great goals to strive for, like the world tournament and the Olympics. Most guys can't go further than Junior hockey. I don't think you'll ever see a woman playing forward in pro hockey with all the body contact . . . only goalies. I think it's almost impossible."

Rick Polutnik, coach of Canada's national team in 1992, says he can tell if the women he coaches have played men's hockey. "The women who have played with males, at least partially during their careers, are generally a little more aggressive. In terms of their reactions they may be a little quicker because the male players force them to move their play up a notch. When they are playing strictly with women, I think sometimes they get away with a few things and it doesn't hurt them. There's no consequence to their error or their slowness. Whereas with males there is. So you do see a bit of a difference with those athletes who have played with males for a significant period of time."

Edmonton's Judy Diduck, a national team member, says there is no reason for women players to compare themselves with men. "I think that just playing at a competitive level and improving satisfies girls. It is very satisfying to play good hockey. After the first world tournament, fans came up to me and said, 'I love watching that kind of hockey. I prefer watching it over guys' hockey.' They said it was pure hockey. The feedback I got was all very positive."

Rebecca Faye of Sackville, New Brunswick, tried out for the national team when she was just 16 years old. Later she played in the inaugural tournament at the Canada Winter Games. Faye says: "My attitude has changed. A couple of years ago, before I knew how big women's hockey really was, and what opportunities there were out there for us, I might have wanted to play in the AHL with Moncton or even in the NHL someday. When you are very young you always think things like that are possible, even though maybe they aren't. Now I'm able to see that there is something to look forward to, like a national team that I can strive to make in the future."

In 1977 the question of whether girls should be allowed to play on boys' hockey teams was presented to the Ontario Human Rights Commission. It had been the hottest topic among the minor hockey leagues for some time, with officials, coaches, parents, and players, as well as the ever-present lawyers, voicing their opinions.

It all began when Dorothy Cummings, the mother of 11-year-old Gail Cummings, lodged a complaint after her daughter was barred from playing goal for a Huntsville (boys) all-star team in the spring of 1977. Gail Cummings was a member of the team simply because there was no comparable girls' team in her community, one that offered competitive hockey at a higher level than house league play. Mrs. Cummings asked the commission to investigate a charge of sex discrimination on the grounds that Gail was denied access to public services and facilities because she was female, a breach of the human rights code. Gail's only comment was: "I don't care if they're boys or girls. I just like to play hockey."

Some hockey officials, worried about the ramifications of mixed teams, launched an appeal. Many threatened to resign if minor hockey became integrated. At the inquiry Dave McMaster, athletic director at St. George's College and head coach of the women's team at the University of Toronto, was asked to testify. "Boys and girls under a certain age, say, 13 or 14, should be able to play sports together without any problems," he told the inquiry. "A person should be able to play at the level of competitiveness that he or she is qualified to play and enjoy. You have to allow young people an equal chance for challenge and growth. I know the hockey association has rules, but maybe the rules aren't good for the kids and they should be changed. We must be more tolerant, more flexible."

The chairperson of the steering committee of the Ontario Women's Hockey Association, lawyer Kay Cartwright, said, "I don't believe children should be separated by sex up to the age of 13. After that the boys are going to become stronger and it's too frustrating for the girls to keep up." Cartwright was supported by the testimony of Abby Hoffman, athlete and sports consultant. Hoffman could speak with firsthand experience. She had been kicked off a male team at the age of eight — for being female.

The board of inquiry ruled that Gail Cummings couldn't be barred from her team on the basis of sex and that the Ontario Minor Hockey Association must allow girls to compete at all levels of play under its jurisdiction — if coaches decided the candidates had the ability. The ruling appeared to be a victory for the Cummings family, but it left several amateur hockey executives shocked and disappointed. The battle proved to be far from over.

"I'm disappointed by the decision," said Gerry Fullan, then president of the Metropolitan Toronto Hockey Association. "To me it's a foolish move." The association announced it would launch an appeal.

With an appeal pending some minor hockey officials went to extremes to maintain a stand. When

Judy Diduck, one of Team Canada '94's best players.

(Ontario Women's Hockey Association)

eight Kitchener, Ontario, teams travelled to Kenosha, Wisconsin, for a tournament against Chicago area teams, nine-year-old Michele Emerson, a girl goalie on the Waukegan, Illinois, team, skated out to play for the Waukegan Shields. But Kitchener refused to take the ice for the opening face-off unless Emerson was replaced. Al Moore, then president of the Ontario Minor Hockey Association, said playing against Emerson would have undermined his association's case in the Ontario Court of Appeal.

When the referee gave the Kitchener team five minutes to ice a team, and they refused to do so, he dropped the puck at centre ice and awarded the game to Waukegan. A Kitchener official said there was no choice in the matter. "If our team had played, our whole league would have been suspended." A subsequent game was played without any fanfare — but with a male goalie replacing Emerson.

The disappointed netminder said: "I knew there was a rule that girls couldn't play on boys' teams in Canada because I had to leave the ice in Sarnia one night. But I didn't think the rule would cover a Canadian team playing in the United States. When I played against Chicago, their players even skated over and gave me some flowers and wished me good luck."

Toronto lawyer Bill McMurtry, who three years earlier headed an investigation into violence in hockey, was surprised by the commission's decision in the Cummings case. "I would question parents who feel their daughters should play against boys," he said. "If girls do play against boys, there should be an age limit, say, 12. It makes no sense to allow girls once past the age of puberty to compete against boys. The physical differences are too great. It would be tough on boys playing against girls. After all, what boy, when he sees a cute little girl skating against him, wants to flatten her with a check? It's wrong. It creates all sorts of problems."

In August 1978 the Divisional Court of the Supreme Court of Ontario, after hearing an appeal from the Ontario Minor Hockey Association, overturned the ruling. Gail Cummings had won her case against the Ontario Minor Hockey Association but had lost in the appeal process. Nine months later the Divisional Court's ruling was appealed to the Ontario Court of Appeal. Months of legal proceedings followed, and by then Gail had lost much of her interest in hockey. She played on the Huntsville all-star lacrosse team and performed well enough as a teenager to be offered a lacrosse scholarship to a Philadelphia college.

John Laskin, lawyer for the Ontario Human Rights Commission, compared the Cummings situation to that of Jackie Robinson, the first black baseball player. "It was only about 30 years ago that a superior black ball player, Jackie Robinson, was able to break into the big leagues, leading to an influx of blacks in baseball. There may be this kind of situation in the present case."

The hockey association lawyer, Wallace Scott of Lindsay, contended the reference to blacks had no place in the case because "Ontario courts ruled against racial discrimination 30 years ago."

Columnist Christie Blatchford, writing in the *Globe and Mail* during the original inquiry, suggested that some officials "reacted like the archaic morons they often are thought to be." She went on to say:

> Many of those officials who spoke at the Commission hearing drew gruesome pictures of how it would be if one little girl was allowed to play. They saw hockey, as they know it, ending. They envisioned herds of little girls showing up at tryout time, imagined the problems of dressing rooms and bathrooms, and panicked. In fact, nothing of the sort would happen. If Canadian girls had wanted to play hockey, there would have been a league for the Huntsville girl to join. But there wasn't, which suggests that most girl-children in Huntsville — and all over Canada — don't really care.
>
> First of all, the question cannot be defined by the case before the Commission. It is not a question of whether girls should be allowed to play on boys' teams; it is one of whether girls should

have equality of opportunity in minor hockey. They should, of course, but the answer isn't necessarily integrated leagues.

On the rare occasions where a talented girl wants to play the game, and where there is no girls' team, she should be allowed to play with the boys. The aim of this would not be to have mixed teams, merely to allow the girl access to the game until a comparable girls' team is formed.

Allowing girls on boys' teams would not result in an increase in the number of girls who want to play. If it did, if hundreds of little girls suddenly decided they wanted to play hockey, then there would be a legitimate demand, and girls' leagues would be formed. This, after all, is how boys' hockey became organized — boys were playing the game in such numbers that organization was necessary. It didn't happen the other way around — leagues were not created first to stimulate interest in the game.

In 1985, after she was barred from playing on a peewee team in Etobicoke, Ontario, 12-year-old Justine Blainey went to the Ontario Human Rights Commission and obtained the legal right to play on a boys' team, as long as she qualified by strength and skill and even if the female team was of a higher calibre than the male team. Her battle lasted four years and went all the way to the Supreme Court of Canada. Attempting to keep her out were the OHA and the OWHA, which spent more than $150,000 in legal fees.

The Human Rights Commission was told that if Blainey played it would be counterproductive to the development of women's hockey in Canada, and expert witnesses outlined extensive opportunities available at that time to Justine within the women's hockey system. In subsequent court proceedings the Divisional Court of Ontario ruled against Blainey, but in 1986 the Ontario Court of Appeal struck down Section 19 (2) of the Ontario Human Rights Code by a 2–1

decision, ruling that sex discrimination in sports was unconstitutional. Mr. Justice Charles Dubin wrote an eloquent dissenting viewpoint.

OWHA president Fran Rider said that Blainey "did, in fact, not have the ability to make some of the stronger female teams. Allowing girls to leave girls' hockey simply because they want to only stigmatizes the female game as second-rate. The best way to advance female hockey opportunities is through unified efforts to develop a parallel stream for girls and women of all ages. In areas where inequalities do exist they should be addressed and corrected to the benefit of everyone."

Eventually Blainey won her case, and the following January she played her first game in a minor bantam league. She played for boys' teams for three years after her case was settled. But her victory came with a cost.

"It became dangerous for me to be alone," she said when she was 19. "I got many calls from men using filthy language. They would say things like, 'You don't deserve to be in this world.' When I went to the arenas, people called me 'Butch' and looked at me funny. Coaches would say, 'You don't belong here.' Then, when I went back to women's hockey, I wasn't welcome. There were a lot of grudges."

The tremendous irony of the Justine Blainey case occurred in 1993 when she was playing for the University of Toronto women's hockey team. The school decided to drop women's hockey despite the fact that the Varsity women had captured 11 of the past 13 Ontario university titles. While the budget of $11,000 for the women's team was lopped, the men's team's budget of $110,000 was left intact. The university seemingly did not recognize the great rebirth of women's hockey. The decision by university officials to deprive some of its finest women athletes of hockey was both shortsighted and sexist. Blainey and others pointed out that men's sports received hundreds of thousands of dollars more than women's sports at the university. But the OWHA and thousands of others rallied behind the Lady Blues and helped save the hockey program for women.

While Blainey's court battles were making headlines in 1986, the Manitoba Amateur Hockey Association, citing a CAHA directive, barred 13-year-old Julie Milne of Letellier, Manitoba, from playing on her local peewee hockey team. But Suzanne Triance, the CAHA's director of female hockey, said it was all a misunderstanding.

"The way we interpret the ruling on the female council is that wherever there is a separate-but-equal hockey program, then girls over the age of 12 should play on the girls' team," Triance said. "However, if a separate-but-equal program doesn't exist, then girls should be permitted to play with the boys, provided they meet the standards of play."

Milne had met all the standards. She was one of the top players on the Emerson Peewees. There were no girls' teams for her to play on near her community in southern Manitoba. Triance also mentioned two 14-year-old girls playing on bantam teams in Medicine Hat, Alberta, and a girl in northern Quebec who was playing Junior B hockey. And in Ontario more than 50 girls were playing on boys' teams with OWHA support.

Other young players were knocking down barriers that once were insurmountable. In 1988 Samantha Holmes of Mississauga became an 11-year-old lobbyist for women's hockey. She attended the Winter Olympic Games in Calgary and was disappointed to learn that no women's teams would be competing. Samantha sat down and wrote letters to everyone from Prime Minister Brian Mulroney to Juan Antonio Samaranch, president of the International Olympic Committee. She wrote:

While I was at the Olympics, I saw six hockey games. I did not see any women's hockey teams. When I get older, I want to be able to compete in hockey with other countries all over the world. I want a chance to stand on a podium and know that I am one of the reasons they are playing 'O Canada.' Will I have that chance? Will other female hockey players have that chance? If not, could you please let me know why? I will try to understand. Also, if the answer is 'no' is there anything you can do to change that? I don't want to give up my dreams.

Samantha Holmes says she has wanted to play hockey since she "was about two years old." When her parents took her skating, she used to kick and cry when it was time to leave the ice. Her parents tried to persuade her to register for the more feminine disciplines like figure skating and ballet. Samantha was five before they gave up and let her play hockey. "From the moment I began playing hockey I refused to ever figure-skate again," she recalls. "All I could think about was going to the Olympics and winning a gold medal as a hockey player. Now the Olympics in Japan are so close I get goose bumps. It's hard to explain how I feel about hockey," she adds. "Whenever I step on the ice it's like the whole world is mine. Even if I'm tired I never want it to end."

Samantha's 1988 plea to politicians and hockey officials didn't fall on deaf ears. She received many replies, mostly urging her not to give up her dreams. Newspapers picked up on her lobbying, and she became an integral part of a feature I helped produce for *Hockey Night in Canada*. In time Samantha developed into such a highly skilled player, as well as being a top student, that she (along with two of her teammates on the Mississauga Chiefs Bantam A championship team) was recruited for an exclusive school in New Hampshire — one with an excellent hockey program for women. At Kimball Union Academy the three young Canadians won't pay a dime of the annual $18,000 tuition. Peter Bartlett, dean of the 180-year-old institution, said: "We have the most competitive high school female hockey in New England. The

Kimball Union program will leave the girls prepared to do well academically in college and help prepare them to play college hockey."

In 1993 Sarah Couch became the first female to play hockey at the junior level in the 103-year history of the Ontario Hockey Association. At 17 Couch played for the Junior C Bowmanville Eagles and was named MVP of the league's all-star game. She wants to play major Junior hockey and aspires to a berth on the women's national team.

"If it hadn't been for Manon Rhéaume, I wouldn't be where I am," she told Lois Kalchman of the *Toronto Star*. Couch sees scouts at her games, but she never knows what they are thinking. "They may be thinking the goalie is pretty good, but she's a girl."

In 1994 Nicole Kirnan, a 13-year-old right winger with the Syracuse Stars, became the first female player in the 13-year history of the Esso Challenge Peewee Hockey Tournament. Kirnan wants to keep playing men's hockey because "it's more challenging and it offers more opportunities in the future." Named *The Hockey News*' minor player of the year in 1990, Kirnan admits the physical challenge is greater as she gets older. And she has to deal with insults from opposing players. "It's true I hear a lot of mean comments from the guys I play against," she says, "but I don't let it bother me."

On May 9, 1994, ALANA PERKINS, a Mississauga mother and first-year player in her thirties, described her first tentative steps into the world of female hockey in the *Toronto Star*:

> As a hockey mother for seven years and a spectator most of my life, I longed to play the game. My first memories were black and white and televised from Maple Leaf Gardens on

Rider Recognized

In May 1994 Fran Rider, executive director of the Ontario Women's Hockey Association, became the first woman to win the Canadian Amateur Hockey Association Order of Merit. Rider, 43, was instrumental in setting up the first women's world hockey tournament in North York, Ontario, in 1987 and was a force in the expansion of women's hockey to official world status through championships in 1990, 1992, and 1994. She also fought hard to have women's hockey recognized as an Olympic sport.

Alana Perkins, a Mississauga mother of two, took up hockey in her mid-thirties. Her linemate, Irene, 65 plus, played back in the Depression.

(Alana Perkins Collection)

a Saturday night. I cheered the speed and finesse of Toronto's teams. I admired many players but did not find any heroes of my own. There were certainly no females hailed.

It's the same situation today when names like Canadian gold medal team member Geraldine Heaney and National Junior Athlete Dawn McGuire fail to receive headlines or the hero worship of National Hockey League players.

Women's hockey has finally been accepted as an Olympic sport and attitudes should change, says Fran Rider, who attributes this year's dramatic leap in player participation from 411 teams last year to the present 557 teams to the Olympics entry in 1998. Across the province, 7,098 female hockey players are taking to the ice with an added incentive. Despite the Olympic recognition, female players remain disadvantaged with no corporate sponsorship.

It wasn't until my second son entered Streetsville minor hockey that I worked up the courage to play. My youngest was six and I was 36. Advantage — mother. In my dreams. He had been deking and

stickhandling since he could toddle. He had grace. I had gliding power and the good fortune to end up on an Etobicoke women's team where grandmothers have been known to face off against grand-daughters and one-third of the players are over 40.

I thought this league was my speed until the first shift and I'm sent out on the wing with Irene. I only get to see her back as she streaks up and down. When we finally go off, I realize Irene is pulling, not pushing, 65. During breathing breaks for me, I heard tales about the Depression when Irene discovered the secret of pain-free shins — strap on the catalogues.

It was three games into the season when I discovered my new skates should have been sharpened after leaving the box. I had been skating on blades with the factory's gummy edge. Since I scored my first goal on those glue pots, my teammates tried to talk me out of sharpening them.

Later I learned it was a non-contact league. Somebody inform my aching back and ankles. For some time I broke many players' falls. A very polite bunch of thugs, always calling "Sorry" after they decked you.

Faceoffs in my end were confusing until the goalie pointed me in the right direction. My first penalty was for politeness and not leaving the ice

The Russians Arrive — Broke and Bewildered

Among the 3,800 women players who gathered in Brampton, Ontario, for the 1994 Canadette Dominion Ladies Tournament were 18 bewildered Russian players and their 10 — yes, 10 — coaches and supporters.

Until the night before the tournament the Russians were stranded in Ottawa with no money and no way to get to Brampton. Their plight reached the ear of Sandra Roy, treasurer of the women's league in Ottawa. She phoned around and arranged for two discounted vans, volunteered to drive one herself, and whisked the Russians to the tournament site in time for the visitors' first game.

The Russian team had been in New York and New Jersey, playing exhibition games in their hopelessly outdated uniforms, when they sought entry to the Canadette tournament. When their money ran out after a bus ride to the Canadian border, they were picked up by members of the Ottawa group and billeted in private homes until Sandra Roy and a friend took over as van drivers.

A team spokesperson said women's hockey is just becoming organized in Russia. Tryouts were held in St. Petersburg and the first national team was chosen. The Russians hope to make a strong showing at the 1998 Olympic Games in Japan.

quickly. In the penalty box, I imagined how my Mississauga mayor, Hazel McCallion (an active OWHA member), would take this. She'd come out with her stick blazing. I did and tripped over another player for another penalty.

Near the season's end, I glanced up at the crowd and saw only five faces. (Two belonged to my sons, with their sign urging "Mum score some.") Hockey is not a spectator sport — when women play.

There are the exceptions, such as the first Women's World Championship in 1990 when Canada won a gold medal before 9,000 and a television audience of over a million. But I find the same story in women's baseball.

As the provinces groom candidates for glory during the training camps this summer and the first women's hockey team to go to the Olympics is assembled, I find myself casually asking the age requirements. Maybe that's the magic of sports. There is always someone to carry forward your dreams.

Can you imagine travelling enormous distances by plane just to play hockey in a place so far north most people have no idea where it is? In 1991 seven women's teams from across the Northwest Territories gathered in Rankin Inlet, a town high on the northwestern coast of Hudson Bay. Fortunately severe storms that had buffeted the area for days subsided by tournament time and all players arrived safely. Most came by plane, others arrived by snowmobile. All of them said they were thankful for the "good" weather — it was minus 35 degrees Celsius.

The tournament was organized by Martha Aupaluktuq, a government worker. Martha bought an old pair of skates when she moved to Rankin from Baker Lake (150 miles away) a few years ago, and she has been playing hockey ever since. "The first thing I saw," she said, "when I entered the new arena they built here in Rankin was some women scraping the ice with pieces of plywood. There was no ice-making machine here then. When the ice was clean, we all began to play."

Most of the women in the tournament brought small children and babies. They wore a type of parka called an *amutiq*, an embroidered garment with a pouch in the hood for carrying infants. The infants were breast-fed between games in the observation room overlooking the ice surface.

The tournament was considered a huge success. Laura Robinson, a *Toronto Star* correspondent, arrived to cover it for the newspaper. She was told the tournament provided an ideal opportunity for the women to get together and find out what was happening in communities separated by hundreds of miles.

The oldest player in the tournament was Jackie King from Coral Harbour. A social worker, King was 41 and a grandmother. She took up hockey after a 15-year absence from skating.

"I have a two-year-old grandson," she said, "and he's already a hockey nut. So we have something in common, something to talk about. I don't even think about my age. I enjoy playing hockey so much. I just love it. I hope this tournament shows the young girls who watch the games and say, 'I wish I could play,' that they can get out and play. It's great exercise."

There were four games played on the final day of the tournament, and when Rankin Inlet won the championship before a standing-room-only crowd, it was said that a number of hibernating bears as far as 50 miles away were awakened by the cheers.

ERIN WHITTEN IS one of three female goaltenders currently playing in men's pro hockey. "I really didn't think about playing professional hockey growing up," she says. "It just kind of popped into my head the past couple of years. I was playing women's hockey at the University of New Hampshire the past four years and I just felt I wanted to continue playing hockey and that's how I got here [Toledo].

"I've seen some changes, some eye-openers, in the attitudes of the men who aren't used to playing with women in hockey. I think with me coming here there have definitely been some changes in attitude and changes in behaviour.

"When I was asked to come here, I talked immediately with Chris McSorley, coach of the Toledo Storm, and he made it clear at the outset that I would not be here as part of a publicity stunt, that I was brought in because I had a chance to make the team. He made it very clear that he did not want me to be part of a media circus. He thought I was a decent goalie who had a chance to be on his team.

"So far I've played in three games. I won two of the games and the other one wasn't my decision.

"I was at the Adirondack Red Wings training camp this year, and that's what led me to Toledo [another Detroit farm team]. But I wasn't really invited there to try out. I was there to get a few practices and get some exposure to pro hockey, although I did end up playing part of an exhibition game. I've already been in the Detroit organization, but there hasn't been any talk about me going to Detroit.

"We play a 68-game season in Toledo, and the coach hasn't given me any idea of how many games I might get in. He has said he'll work me in as much as he can without hurting the chances of his team to win. I'm a young, underdeveloped goalie right now with a lot of development to go. So my whole purpose is to develop myself and work hard.

"The fans have been very positive in their support. The fans here are great. They cheer me during warm-ups. They cheer every save I make. I couldn't ask for better support.

"As for playing for a team in the NHL someday, that's a long-term goal. I'd love to do it. I'd absolutely love to. But I've got a lot of development to do yet.

"I've had to slash a few calves and ankles in my day. Every goalie has to do it. But I've got a lot of work to do and these guys are much bigger than the players I'm used to playing against."

Of course, if Erin Whitten ever plays against Manon Rhéaume, it would be a hockey first.

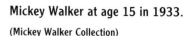

IN 1993 I WAS INVITED to take part in an exhibition game (yes, as a player) during the Brampton Canadettes annual tournament. When they told me I would be playing on the same team, perhaps on the same line, as Mickey Walker, I readily agreed to don my skates. Why? Because Mickey Walker is one of the true legends of women's hockey. At 76 she still plays weekly games in Bala, Ontario. Since our first meeting, we have become good friends. The following is part of Mickey's story, recorded after our game in Brampton.

"All the members of my family were good athletes, no matter what the sport. And my mother was a beautiful skater. I was born right beside Lake Muskoka, so there was always ice in the winter to skate on. One of the first places I ever played hockey was on an outdoor rink. There was a little shack nearby with a potbellied stove inside. The snow was so high it came over the boards to the point you couldn't see them. In an interview with Bill McNeil on the CBC program *Fresh Air*, I told him about the hand-me-down equipment we wore, the condition of my skates, and how one year my toes stuck out through a hole in one of my skates. My skates were sharpened by my dad on an old grindstone. You won't see anything like that today. My dad could do anything with his hands. I had to use old hand-me-down sticks, even though a new stick cost only 25 cents. The first team I played for was the Bala girls' team. We had only an hour a week for practice. It was after school on Friday afternoon at four o'clock.

"I couldn't wait for those practices. So on Friday afternoon in class, at about three-thirty, I'd turn around and start to talk to someone. The teacher — he called me Mary — would catch me and he'd say, 'Mary Walker — out!' And I'd have to leave class. Well, I'd gather up my things and run down the street and be at the arena long before my friends showed up. Then one day the principal saw me hurrying along with my skates and stick, and the next time I talked in class, hoping to be let out early, the teacher said, 'Mary Walker — you stay after class for half an hour.' Well, that cured me. I never tried my little trick to get to the arena early ever again.

"I played for Bala and I played for Bracebridge and I played for Gravenhurst. In Bracebridge Kit Ecclestone, one of the older girls, took one look at my old skates and marched me down to her dad's hardware store. He handed me a new pair of CCM skates worth $5. They were the first new skates I'd ever owned. We had such good teams in those days. Twice we played the Preston Rivulettes, the greatest team in Canada. I was a little stagestruck, frankly, because the arena was packed with fans. Our girls had never seen so many people at a hockey game. We lost in 1934 by 3–1, and the following year I joined the Gravenhurst team for another crack at them. It was late in the season and there was about an inch of water on the Preston ice — not a good surface for a stickhandler.

Mickey Walker in 1993, 75 years young.
(Mickey Walker Collection)

"When big Marm Schmuck came at me, my brother Reg yelled, 'Step into her, Mickey,' and I did. Marm went down, but her stick clipped me on the nose and I soon had two black eyes as souvenirs. To add to my problems, a woman spectator tried to swat me on the head with her umbrella whenever I got within range. I believe we lost 9–1.

"I've made lifelong friends over the years while playing with all the different girls on all the different teams. I still try to keep in touch with as many as possible.

"I played centre all through my career, and while I don't get around the ice like I used to, I still enjoy playing the game to this day. I've had the same hockey stockings for 35 years, and I always wear CCM equipment. Whenever possible I wear my number 99 jersey. A few years ago I went out to buy a pair of skates and I couldn't believe that some of them cost $200.

"Bill McNeil was a little concerned when he interviewed me on the CBC. He told me if I used a swear word he could always edit it from the tape. I told him not to worry — I wouldn't swear because I'm a lady first and a hockey player second.

"I abhor violence in the game. I pray that violence never comes into women's hockey because it would be a disgrace. See the sparkle in my eye when I talk about violence? I was going to sit down and write a letter to that man, Don Cherry. I was so upset I couldn't get the words down. I can't tolerate Mr. Cherry on television because it seems to me all he ever does is promote violence. I hate violence in hockey. The good players are being put out of the game by these, these . . . goons! They can't play the game. They're just out there to hurt someone. Then Mr. Cherry makes videos out of it and makes millions! Oh, my goodness, it upsets me. I see the message seeping down to the kids I work with. Imagine little ones 10 years old getting violent on the ice. Sometimes their parents send them to me and I have a talk with them. They'll say, 'We're sorry we lost our cool' and 'We'll try not to do it again.'

"I'm just so happy about our sport today that I'm almost bursting. The girls have worked so hard and come so far. Just look at the results!"

Provocative Assertions by Ph.D

In 1991 Aniko Varpalotai, Ph.D., wrote a provocative article focusing on girls' sports and role models. Some of Dr. Varpalotai's observations included:

Research in education has shown that girls benefit from single-sex educational environments while coeducation favours boys.

Why would girls prefer to play on all-girls' teams? Boys become rougher as they get older and they resent a girl who is a better player than they are. The girl is then compelled to accept the "female frailty" myth and adjust herself accordingly (i.e., not try as hard in order to save the boy from embarrassment).

Limited integration during preadolescence was considered acceptable and perhaps even good, but the preference on the whole was for single-sex sporting opportunities, regardless of the sport.

Young girls currently playing ringette all reported a desire to play hockey when they were younger but recalled being redirected by parents or others to a more "suitable" sport for girls, usually figure skating.

There appears to be a contradiction in maintaining single-sex organizations for girls and women in an era when women are trying hard to break into previously all-male enclaves in education, the workplace, unions, and other organizations. At the same time studies of girls' and women's education are telling us that girls learn better in a single-sex environment, and indeed, many girls prefer and enjoy time spent with other girls and women.

When girls are offered opportunities to participate in a sport of their own, they manage to excel. Interaction with female leaders and instructors encourages them to develop leadership skills of their own.

When I asked Mickey to send me a photo of her playing hockey at a young age, she sent me a beauty. She told me once: "Some time ago I ran into a man who was a childhood friend of mine. I hadn't seen this man in decades. He took me aside and said, 'Look, Mickey, see what I've carried in my wallet for almost 60 years. It's a photo of you.' Now isn't that flattering?"

Mickey Walker is the oldest woman playing hockey in Canada. She's a gem!

Mabel Boyd of Mississauga, 72, is a hockey legend. Not even Gordie Howe can claim to have two sons, three grandsons, a sister, a niece, and a granddaughter all playing hockey. And a great-granddaughter ready to don her first pair of skates.

Mabel is a pioneer in women's hockey. In 1967 she helped form the first women's league in Mississauga. She has also helped organize many tournaments for women and competed in several herself — at an age when many of her contemporaries are content to sit at home watching the soaps.

In the early seventies, representing the Mississauga Indians, she played in tournaments in Finland (twice), Holland, Germany, and England. In 1989 a sports magazine called her for an interview, but she had little time to talk. She was busy packing for a trip to Vancouver. Seems her kid sister, Margaret Offer, age 53, was playing in a tournament, and Mabel wanted to be there to cheer her on. A few weeks later Mabel was recruited for a trip to Hawaii — not to absorb some rays on Waikiki Beach, but to don her skates and play in another hockey tournament. "They have an ice rink in Hawaii?" she was asked on her return.

In 1991 Mabel organized a new league — the Mississauga Women's Masters League — for women over

35. And two years ago Mabel and Mickey Walker faced off against each other in the Huntsville Honeys tournament. Both captained their respective teams, and their combined ages totalled 144 years. Mabel is the oldest officially registered female hockey player in Canada, and she still gets a kick out of playing against the "kids" in her Masters League.

When players half her age talk about their hockey heroes and names like Wayne Gretzky, Doug Gilmour, and Patrick Roy slip off their tongues, Mabel just smiles. Her childhood hero was Charlie Conacher of the Leafs. He was a big star in the thirties and retired in 1941, long before any of her teammates were born.

GEORGINA RAYNER, who grew up in Kenora, Ontario, has done research into women's sports in Canada. She played hockey for the University of Guelph in the 1960s. The following are some excerpts from an interview I did with her at the Brampton Canadettes tournament in 1993.

"Almost anyone with an interest in sport could play on a women's team in university. But when it came to hockey you had to have your own equipment. So I ran out and bought some skates and other equipment and played on the women's university team for a full four years. Most of our games were against the women from Queen's and McGill.

"In those days we were instructed by our coaches and managers to promote the game with dignity. For example, we were not allowed to swear or argue with the officials in any way. The women's team at Guelph used to play exhibition games against the men's club on the campus. No rough play or body contact was allowed. Believe it or not, once we tied the men's team 10 all.

"I fancied myself as a basketball player when I entered Guelph, but when I went into the gym and saw all these girls wearing short skirts, I balked. Coming from the north country, I couldn't imagine myself wearing one of those skirts. So I walked right through the building and into the hockey rink and was amazed to see women on the ice — with sticks and a puck! I couldn't believe it. I asked Shirley Peterson, the coach, 'Is this a women's team?' She said, 'Yes.' I asked, 'Can anyone play?' She replied, 'You have to have your own skates.' So I ran out and jumped on the bus, went downtown, and bought a pair of skates. Then I raced back to the university, jumped on the ice, and played on the women's team there for the next four years.

"Back home I grew up with five brothers, and we played pickup games on the river. Girls weren't allowed to play hockey in Kenora. In the north country girls were allowed to curl. So we were curlers. But I would have killed to play hockey as a youngster.

"There was a great university league when I played at Guelph. And we had a very strong team when I was there. In some of our games, especially against teams like Queen's, we would score a few goals at the start. Then Shirley would insist that we had to make so many passes before we'd take a shot on goal. That way we didn't build up a huge score. Then in the third period, she'd say, 'Fill the net.'

"She taught us something very important about hockey. She said, 'Girls, you are women first and hockey players second.' She said the way to promote the sport was to promote it with dignity. No matter where we went we always dressed in skirts and blazers. She wouldn't tolerate a foul mouth. She didn't want to put across an image that we were anything but well-behaved athletes. She really taught respect. It is something that most of us involved with hockey today pass along to our players. In the league that I run there's zero tolerance for swearing. I tell the girls that hockey is for fun. You're not going to be respected if you use foul language and put on a poor image.

"One year at Guelph, when our team was rebuilding, a Toronto team coached by Dave McMaster had us down 4–1 with a minute left to play. One of my teammates accused me of lying down and allowing a goal. I was so cross I threw my stick at my own team and was given a 10-minute misconduct. Well, Dave's team made the mistake of giving me a standing ovation as I left the ice. My teammate — the girl who had made the comment I objected to — became so cross and so inspired that she took the puck and scored three goals to tie the score. In the overtime we scored again to win the game — with 15 seconds left to play!

"At Guelph, during minor hockey week, we played some exhibition games against men's teams. Now we had some tremendous hockey players at that time and we played the Junior A team in Guelph. We had certain rules — no slap shots and no bodychecking. And with two minutes left to play in the game, we were winning! That's when the boys lost their cool. They got mad. The slap shots started flying in, the bodychecks knocked us to the ice, and they tied the score. But the fans were irate. They booed the Juniors off the ice for being such poor sports. The boys had to be ashamed. They had no idea that girls could play hockey that well.

"We played one day at a small farm community. It was a fund-raiser. I remember getting off the bus and the local kids gathered around. We were all dressed up in our high boots and nice clothes. And two or three of the girls were really spiffy-looking women. Well, the local boys gathered around and they were laughing and joking and making smart remarks about our abilities as hockey players.

"As soon as we put on our hockey gear, we were terrors. We put on a show that day and silenced those quipsters. They couldn't believe we could play hockey as well as we did."

Mickey Walker, Mabel Boyd, and Georgina Rayner are just a few of the many wonderful women who played Canada's national game in bygone years. Their dedication, determination, and sheer love of the sport can only serve as an inspiration to the thousands of young girls now enrolling in hockey schools and joining leagues across the country. The future is indeed bright.

Epilogue

WOMEN HAVE INVADED and become successful in areas that once were considered "male only." Most women seek the joy of competition, the pleasure that comes from learning new skills. Most are late starters, taking up activities like weight training, running, cycling, and team sports such as basketball, softball, volleyball, and hockey. Those who were in high school in the sixties and early seventies, when they attended sports events "to cheer, not to play," recall getting little encouragement to become participants.

For decades young women have been told "Don't be a tomboy." They have been told that boys are naturally superior athletes, and if a girl does possess athletic skills, it may not be wise to "show up the boys" by demonstrating her athleticism. Girls have been told that "muscles are unattractive," that "you can't compete because you're too small, you're not strong enough, you might get hurt."

Size and strength may be important factors in basketball and football, but in hockey they are both overrated, especially in women's hockey which, unlike the men's game, is devoid of goons and enforcers. Stickhandling and passing skills are more important than strength, and small players with a low centre of gravity are often much better skaters than tall, strong players. What women lack in strength, some athletes contend, they make up for in endurance and toughness. If women can deal with the stress and pain of childbirth, an experience that requires mental and physical toughness, they can deal with anything that happens in a hockey rink. They have, in a word, guts.

More and more young girls are lacing on skates and taking up sticks to play Canada's national game. Here is the gold medal-winning team in the National Under 18 Women's Hockey Championship at Loyola Campus, Concordia University, Montreal, in February 1993.

(Ontario Women's Hockey Association)

Young women need heroes. It is easy for girls to idolize Patrick Roy, Doug Gilmour, or Wayne Gretzky — young women will always have male heroes. But they also need female heroes (does anyone call them heroines anymore?). Goaltender Cathy Phillips is an outstanding role model for young female hockey players. Others are Angela James, Dawn McGuire, Geraldine Heaney, and France St. Louis.

Women also want more of a voice in how women's sports programs are administered and how young women are coached and guided. Numerous studies show that female leaders tend to be less autocractic than male leaders. Charol Shakeshaft, an associate professor of administration and policy studies at Hofstra University, wrote in 1986: "Female administrators spend more time with people, communicate more, care more about individual differences, are more concerned with other teachers and with marginal students, and are better motivators than men."

There would be many more women coaches and administrators if it wasn't for the difficulty of combining marriage and career. A U.S. college survey reveals that 93 percent of male college coaches are married and 80 percent have children. Only 35 percent of women coaches are married and only 16 percent are mothers. One female college athletic director said: "Women don't have the mobility men do. A woman coach might be offered a good job only to have her husband say, 'That's great but we're not moving.' His job comes first. And some men can't cope with their wives as head coaches. The divorce rate in this department is high."

It is unfortunate more women aren't involved in coaching and administration. Most women agree that women's sports, dominated for years everywhere but on the playing field itself by males, should be administered, coached, and officiated by women. In hockey women coaches and game officials, with a sensitivity rarely found in men's sport, can help establish new attitudes and approaches to the game.

In the NHL and other leagues there is a "win or else" ethic. A coach wins or he is replaced. Players produce or they are gone. Violence is "part of the game," and enforcers who can intimidate (beat up) opposing players are valued team members. Judging by the attitudes of females, coaches and players alike, involved in Canada's national team program, and women hockey players from other countries, it appears that women have adopted a refreshingly different, certainly more civilized attitude toward hockey and other sports. The focus remains on winning, but not at any price. Competitors are quick to show respect and tolerance for their opponents. They are not so much foes and enemies as they are comrades and allies. They appear to care about their rivals and cherish the concept of team togetherness and the enjoyment of the match. And they care about themselves and the image they project.

With their newfound confidence they now look for new fields to conquer. It is hoped they will penetrate the male domains of coaching and administration. More than half of all women's college teams in the United States are still coached by men. Of the 105 members of the U.S. Olympic Committee, 91 are men. In 1991, of the 38 national governing bodies of sport in the United States, 34 were presided over by men. In Canada, where statistics are not as readily available, it is assumed the lopsided numbers in favour of males are similar.

The head coaches of the three IIHF World Championship teams in women's hockey were men — Dave McMaster (1990), Rick Polutnik (1992), and Les Lawton (1994). It is time for women to step forward and replace men in positions of responsibility in women's hockey. The glamour job is coaching, but there is a need for competent managers, instructors, trainers, referees, goal judges, scorekeepers, and timekeepers.

In the sixties former Toronto Maple Leaf president Harold Ballard barred women reporters from the press box at Maple Leaf Gardens. When I became involved in a heated discussion with him over this policy, he barked at me, "Let's get one thing straight, McFarlane. There'll be no bleepin' women in the press box!" And he stalked off. Since then women reporters have become a large presence in the world of hockey journalism, and they have access not only to press boxes but dressing rooms, as well.

Why is it that a woman hasn't established herself as the unofficial historian of women's hockey? If one had, it would be appropriate for her to be the chronicler of the history of the game — more appropriate than for me to be compiling these pages, although I make no apology for my involvement. It has been a highly satisfying experience.

In the sixties *Hockey Night in Canada* hired Helen Hutchinson, then with *Canada AM* on CTV, as a between-periods interviewer. Hutchinson's limited knowledge of the game and the people in it resulted in intermission chats that were banal and uninspired. She was let go after one season. The producers might well have offered the position to a more dedicated, ambitious woman, one with a genuine love for the game. Such a woman might well be with the program today. And surely, somewhere, there is a woman with a burning ambition to become a female counterpart to Bob Cole or Dick Irvin, calling play-by-play of women's games at future world championships and the Olympics. Why not? Especially since recent surveys reveal that women are watching hockey on TV in record numbers. The Ottawa Senators learned through their latest audience research that women make up close to 40 percent of their total viewership.

In her splendid book *Are We Winning Yet: How Women Are Changing Sports and Sports Are Changing Women*, author Mariah Burton Nelson, a former professional basketball star, states:

You can't be a female athlete without addressing questions of femininity, sexuality, fear, power, freedom and just how good you are compared with men. In the complex, contradictory world of women's sports, female athletes want a piece of the male pie one day and serve an all-female pudding the next. They wear crop-tops to look sexy for a bicycling date, then pedal home alone hoping not to attract heckling or worse. The paradoxes can be paralyzing, but they yield tenacious women who are dedicated not only to breaking athletic and cultural barriers but also to helping other women along the way.

Nelson writes of women crouched at the starting blocks, ready to sprint toward equal opportunity, and how more women and girls play sports, particularly highly competitive ones, than ever before.

> What has this meant for women? They are getting pleasure out of sheer physical competence. They are taking physical risks, and having fun in the process. Women athletes now have female stars to model themselves after, and those stars are gaining more fame and fortune than would have been thought possible twenty years ago. Sports participation has given millions of women new self-confidence and has taken them to where they never were before onto what used to be male turf.

Sometime during the nineties a North American professional league may beckon today's talented young women players. Certainly the rapid evolution of the game, especially over the past decade, has dazzled those who have witnessed it or been a part of it. At the 1998 Olympics in Japan a display of relentless puck chasing at high speed, creative individual skills, and clever team play will draw the attention of a world audience, including wealthy entrepreneurs and promoters. The competitors will provide a high degree of entertainment and reap an equal amount of respect. The ramifications — the impact on the hearts and minds of young women everywhere — will be felt long into the next century.

Index

Abby Hoffman Cup, 139, *140*, 144
Aces Hockey League (Montreal), 127–28
administration, women in, 198, 199
Agincourt Canadians, 140
Agnew, Dave, 124–25
Aikens, Jean, 94
Allan, Janet, 62, 63, 66
Allen, Janet, 29
Amateur Athletic Union of Canada, 45
American Athletic Union, 82
American Hockey Association, 133
Andreason, Ellen, 60
arenas, 11, 13, 17, 55, 56
assault charges, 148
Atkinson, Jean, 108
Ault, Eva, *50*, 61
Aupaluktuq, Martha, 185–86

Ballard, Harold, 199
Banff, Alberta, games, 17, *46*, 58
Banwell, Trudy, 148
Barr, Olive, 68
Barrie, Ontario, match in 1892, 18
Bartlett, Peter, 181–82
Beattie Ramsay Trophy, 58
Beaudry, Yves, 167
Belleville Scorchers, 29
Bennett, "Sis," 93
Black Cats of Haileybury, 83
Black, Marjorie, 90
Blainey, Justine, 178–80
Blair, May, 21, 22
Blatchford, Christie, 177–78
bloomers, 49, *50*
bodychecking, 29, 30, 61, 86, 111, 131, 132, 147, 153, 161

Boston Massport Jets, 131
Boyd, Mabel, 154, 192–93
Boyd, Stephanie, 156
Brampton Canadettes, 122
Bresbois, Louise, 47
Broda, Turk, 115–16
Bush, Joey, 147
Bush, President George, 153–54

Calgary Grills, 95–97
Calgary Hollies, 58
Cameron, Shirley, 139–40
Campbell, Cassie, *160*
Campbell, Clarence, 99, 126
Campeau, Barb, 130
Canada Games, 149
Canadian Amateur Hockey Association, 3, 102, 137, 138, 139, 149, 156
Canadian championship (1930s), 85–86, 90, 91–93, 102, 103, 108
Canadian Polish Athletic Club, 142
Canadian Women's Hockey Association, 86, 92
Card, Anson, 23
Carleton Place team, 24
Cartwright, Katherine "Cookie," 124, 128–34,
Cartwright, Kay, 175
Case, Mary, 86
Catherwood, Ethel, 58, 61
Catherwood, Genevra "Ginger," 58, 60, 61
Caucheon, Simone, 82
Chalk River team, 71
Champion–Demers, Frank, 137–38
Charette, Pierre, *167*
Charlottetown Abbie Sisters, 102
Charlottetown Islanders, 102, 103

Cherry, Don, 190
chest protectors, 26, 54
Clancy, King, 138
Clark, Toots, 94
coaches, women as, 198–99
Cobalt Marvels, 101
Cobalt, Ontario, men's hockey in, 37, 39
Cobalt, Ontario, women's hockey in, 38, 39–43
Cobalt Silver Belles, 126
Concordia University, 142
Connell, Joan, 122
Cook, Myrtle, 74, 82–83, 89, 92, 95–96
Copping, Margie, 116
Cornell, Ward, 123
Cornwall Vics, 36–37
costumes, 14, 16, 18, 26, 30, 34, 39, 45, 53, 115, 122, 152
Couch, Sarah, 182
Coutts, Jim, 134
Coveny, Marion, *136*, 147–48
Creelman, Alex, 21, 22
Crystal Sisters, 89, 91
Cummings, Dorothy, 174
Cummings, Gail, 174, 175, 176–77

Dalhousie University team, *106*
Danielson, Line, 145
Davidson, Melody, 162
Dawson City Nuggets (male players), 12–13
Dawson City women's games, *11*, 12
declining interest in 1940s, 107–110
Diduck, Judy, 152, 163, 173, 175
Domes, Mrs. Art McCann, 115
Dominion Ladies Hockey Tournament, 122, 184, 188
Dominion Women's Amateur Hockey Association, 95, 96, 97
Don Mills Satan's Angels, 124

Drolet, Nancy, 160–61
Dryden, Sarah, 157, *158*
Dyer, Kelly, 2, 153, 164
Dykeman, M. J., 96

Eagleson, Alan, 139
Edmonton Chimos, 140
Edmonton Grads basketball team, *48*, 49, 77
Edmonton Monarchs, 58, *80*
Edmonton Rustlers, 84, 85–86, 90
Edmonton teams, 13, *19*, 58
Edmonton teams, Victoria High School Team, *59*
Emerson, Michele, 176
equipment, 26, 53–54, 111, 113, 129
Eruzione, Mike, 166
Esposito, Phil, 169

face mask, 70
fans, *see* spectators
Faye, Rebecca, 173
females on male teams, 172–80, 182
Fenwick, Marjorie, 64
Ferguson, Kim, 130–31
Fichtenbaum, Paul, 153
Fiddie, Sylvie, 94
fights, 36, 41–42, 91–92, 94, 102, 125, 130–31
financial support, 111–12
first known women's league (1900), 16
first-ever women's hockey match, 4, 9, 17–18
Flood, Brian, 13
Forest team, 66, 67
Forrest, Albert, 13
Forrest, Evelyn, 13
Fowler, Pat, 130
Francis, Val, 87
Fulford, Robert, 74
Fullan, Gerry, 175

Gallant, Connie, 113–14
gate receipts, 96, 97, 98–99
Gaudet, Albert, 102
Gault, Maureen, 97, 98
Gerow, Janean, 130, 133
Gibb, Alexandrine, 5, 68–69, 70, 86–87, 90, 92, 98–99, 100, 101, 102, 108
Giles, Marion, 61, 64
Ginzel, Heather, 161

goaltenders, 2, 30, 40, *54*, 64, 66, 67, 68, 70, 84–85, 91, 92, 133, 140, 157–58, 164, 167–71, 186–87
Gooding, Ruby, 67
Goodlands Starettes, 132
Gowland, Vida, 69, 71, 83, 85
Goyette, Danielle, *160*, 166
Grady, Lynnie Gallant, 112–14
Graham, Elizabeth, 70
Granato, Cammi, 166
Greene, Nancy, 139
Gretzky, Wayne, 166
Griffiths, Phyllis, 56, 73, 83, 84, 86
Grnak, Marianne, 2, *163*
Guelph, Ontario, players, 24
Guidolin, Bep, 107
Gurley, Helen, 49, 56
Gwyn, Sandra, 22
Gyde, Wanda, 133

Hackett, Alice, 69
Haggerty, Jackie, 145
Haileybury, Ontario, men's hockey, 37, 39
Haileybury, Ontario, women's hockey, 35, 39–43, 83
hair, 92
Hamilton Golden Hawks, 144–45
Hamilton, Marjorie, 29
handicapped players, 141
Harley, Lynda, 140
Harper, Henry, 21, 22
Heaney, Geraldine, 2, 152–53, 163, 198
Hebert, Karen, 145
Herbie Hoare Trophy, 94
Hewitt, Bill, 123
Hilliard, Marian, 55, 56, *63*, 64, 67
Hipel, Norma, 99
Hiscock, Marie, 26
Hoban, Margaret, 102
Hockey Hall of Fame, 139
Hockey Night in Canada, 181, 201
Hoffman, Abigail, 117–19, 137–38, *140*, 155, 172, 175
Holmes, Samantha, 154–56, *157*, 180–82
Hutchinson, Helen, 201
Hutchinson, Theresa, 155

intercollegiate play, 54, 58, 60, 67, 87, 116, 121, 129, 131
International Ice Hockey Federation, 4, 143

James, Angela, *146*, 155, 162, 164, 166, 172, 198
Janneau, Françoise, 127, 128
Jenish, D'arcy, 152
Jenkins, Kathleen, 51
Jones, Nellie, 69, 94

Kalchman, Lois, 147, 148, 182
Kananites (Nova Scotia club), *14*
Kay, Karen, 166
King, Jackie, 186
Kingston Aerials, 29
Kingston Red Barons, 130
Kirnan, Nicole, 182
Koch, Patty, 141
Koelnel, Pauline Sweeney, 103
Kohen, Colleen, 147
Kolt, Tommy, 95, 97

Ladies' Ontario Hockey Association, 54, 58, 62–63, 64, 66, 82, 97
Lady Bessborough Trophy, 90, 91, 92–93, 97, 98
Lady Brenda Meredith Trophy, 94
Lambert, Yvette, 91
Lambton Ladies, 130
Lapansee, Albertine, 36–37
Laskin, John, 177
Latner, Anita, 118–19
Lawton, Les, 162, 163, 164, 199
Lazerenko, Harry, 129, 147
Leah, Vince, 109–110
Leeman, Rhonda, 130
Lemoine, Lulu, 20–21
Les Canadiennes, 93
liquor, 114
Locke, Norma, 101
Lockhart, Lloyd, 115–16
London team, 66
Lucan Leprechauns, 125–26
Lumsden, Barb Austin, 132
Lumsden, Margaret, 91
Lytle, Andy, 49, 78–79

McCallion World Cup, *136*, 144
McCallion, Hazel, 110–12, *136*, 143, 157, 185
McCauley, Dwight, 132
McFadden, Roxann, 123
McFarlane, Brian, 123, 188, 199

McGill University players, 14–15, 27, 54, 58, 121, 129, 142
McGuire, Dawn, 140, 148, 153, 172, 198
McIlroy, Thora, 64
McInnes, Miss, 102
McKay, Elva, *71*
McLean, Casey, 66, 67
McLeod, Don, 153, 154, 155
McMaster, Dave, 148, 152, 154, 174–75, 194, 199
McMaster University, 129
McMurtry, Bill, 176
McNeil, Bill, 188, 190
McPharland, "Mac," 40
McSorley, Chris, 187
McTeer, Maureen, 137–38, 139, *140*
Magnussen, Karen, 139
Manitoba Amateur Hockey Association, 180
Manson, May, 91, 103
Meagher, George, 21
Medicine Hat, Alberta, teams, 13, 17, 58
Melfort Missilettes, 141
men's team defeated by women, 47
Mews, Olive, 64
Meyers, Miss (Cobalt player), 41, 42
Miller, Annie, 64, 66, 68, 82
Miller, Shannon, 162
Mills, Thora, 53–54
Milne, Julie, 180
Milne, Lucy, 63
Minto, Lady, 20, 21, 23
Minto, Lord, 21–23
Mississauga Women's Masters League, 192–93
Montour, France, 155
Montreal Maroons, 89, 93, 94
Montreal teams, from 1962, *120*
Montreal teams, from early 1900s, *15*, 16
Montreal Titans, 142
Moody, Maryon, 54
Moore, Al, 176
Moore, Dolly, 94
Moose Jaw Wildcats, 114–15
Morris, Roy, 122
Moulds, Shirley, *60*, 61, 62, 64, 66, 67
Mowers, Johnny, 124
Murphy, Mereida Roach, *104*
Murray, Debbie, 130

National Hockey Association, 37, 39

National Hockey League, 107, 198
National Hockey League, first woman to play in, *see*
    Rhéaume, Manon
National Under 18 Women's Hockey Championship, *196*
Nattrass, Susan, 139
Nelson, Mariah Burton, 201–202
Nicholas, Cindy, 139
Nicholl, Pat, 124
Nicholson, Big Billy, 39, 40, 93
Nicholson, Helen, 39, 93, 94, 95
nicknames for teams, 27
North American Girls Hockey Championship, 124, 132
North Battleford Sweetheart Tournament, 141
North Toronto Ladies team, 61, 62, 63
North Vancouver Dynamos, 141
Norwegian Ice Hockey Federation, 4
number of players today, 4
Nystrom, Karen, *146*, *163*

O'Brien Trophy, 39
Offer, Margaret, 192
Ogrean, David, *174*
O'Hara, Jane, 152
Oke, Teddy, 61
Olympic Games, 2, 4, 133–34, 135, 149, 162, 180–81, 202
Ontario Agricultural College, 121
Ontario Hockey Association, 178, 182
Ontario Human Rights Commission, 174, 178
Ontario Minor Hockey Association, 175, 176
Ontario Women's Hockey Association, 134, 137, 138, 142,
    143, 149, 156
Ormsby, Mary, 156, 162, 170–71
Ottawa, first written account of game (1891), 4, 17–18
Ottawa Alerts, 54, *60*, 61, 62, 63–64, 70
Ottawa Alpha Ladies Club, 18, 20
Ottawa Rangers, 101
Ottawa Rowing Club, 64, *65*, 66, 67, 83
Ottawa Solloway–Mills, *68*, 69
Owen Sound, Ontario, team in late 1890s, *22*

Page, Margot Verlaan, *4*, 155, 156, 163
Page, Percy, 49
Parks, Marie, 56, 58
penalties, 27, 29, 42, 70, 90, 91, 93, 102, 166
Perkins, Alana, 182–85
Peters, Glynis, 161, 162
Peterson, Shirley, 194

Petty, Dini, 161
Phillips, Cathy, *136*, 140, 145, 148, 154, 157, *158*, 172, 198
photograph, earliest known of women players, *6*, 10
pioneer women, 33
Pitcher, Gladys Hawkins, 86, 94, 102, 103
Polutnik, Rick, 161, 173, 199
Port Arthur Bearcats, 114
Port Dover Sailorettes, 87–88
Poste, Marg, 122
Potter, Leila Brooks, 77
Pounder, Cheryl, *163*
Preston Golden Trianglettes, 121
Preston, Ontario teams, 63, 71
Preston Rivulettes, 2–3, *76*, 83, 84, 85–86, 89–99, 100,
    101–103, 104, 108, 189
Prince Albert Girls Hockey League, 141
Prince Edward Island Amateur Hockey Association, 142
professional warnings about sports, 47

Quebec Amateur Hockey Association, 128
Quebec Ice Hockey Federation
Quebec Ladies Hockey Club (1900), 24
Quebec Northern Electrics, 82
Quebec provincial championships, 142
Queen's University teams, 16, 18, 54, 56, 58, 67, 70, 87,
    121, 128–29

radio play-by-play account, 132
Rankin Inlet, N.W.T., tournament, 185–86
Ranscombe, Hilda, 85, 90, 94, 97, 100, 102, 103, 108, 121,
    127
Ranscombe, Nellie, 85, 92
Ransom, Helen, 92
Rayner, Georgina, 193–95
referee, 15, 42, 64, 67, 69–70, 98, 102, 126
Regina teams, *12*, 23
Reid, Maurice "Lefty," 139
Reid, Pat, 153
Renwick, Gordon, 162
Rhéaume, Manon, 2, 4, 160–61, 164, 167–71, 172, 187
Ribson, Harold, 122–23, 125–27
Ribson, Lila, 122–23, 125–27
Rider, Fran, 134–35, 143, *146*, 162, 172, 179, 182, 183
Robinson, Jackie, 177
Robinson, Laura, 186
Rocky Mountain Park Trophy, 58
Roffey, Dot, 66, 83

Romeo Daoust Trophy, 90, 94
Rosenfeld, Bobbie, 56, 62, 63, 64, 66, 67, 68, 73–74, 75, 78, 79, 81–82, 83, 85, 97, 108
Ross, Doris, 64, 66
Ross, Marion, 128, 129
rough play, 30, 36, 40, 41–42, 55, 61–62, 86, 91–92, 94, 108, 125, 130–32, 190, 198–99
Rouse, Allen
Roverines of Newfoundland, 104, *105*
Roxborough, Henry, 27, 78
Roy, Sandra, 184
rules, 128, 131, 195
Runions, Ernie, 36, 37
Russia, 184

Saint John players, 13–14
Saint John Women's Hockey League, 142
St. John's Ladies Hockey League, 142
St. Louis, France, 152, 153, 162, 166, 172–73, *174*, 198
Salming, Borje, 145
Saskatchewan, women's hockey (1890s–1910s), 24, 26–27
Saskatchewan Ladies Hockey League, 141
Saskies, 141
Scherer, Sue, 130, 131, 151, 159–60, 161
Schmuck, Helen, 83, *85*, 91
Schmuck, Marm, 85, 92, 94, 97, 102, 103, 190
Scott, Wallace, 177
"seaming," 104
Shakeshaft, Charol, 198
Sharp, Jean, 30
Shibicky, Alex, 98
Shibicky, Anne, 98
shinny, 24, *25*, 26
Shoppers Drug Mart Women's National Hockey Championship, 137–41
Simpson, Winnie, 66
Sittler, Meaghan, 157, *158*
skates, 55, 113, 115–16, 132
skating for women, 50–51, *52, 53*
Smith, Neil, 98
Smythe, Conn, 109
Sorge, Wolfgang, 149
South King's County, P.E.I. team. 102
spectators, 16–17, 18, 20, 30, 36, 37, 39, 42, 61, 86, 90, 91, 92, 96, 98, 100, 104, 185, 187, 201
sponsors, 109, 112, 138
Sports Canada, 138

Stanley Cup, 1, 7, 10
Stanley, Isobel (Lady Isobel Gathorne–Hardy), *6*, 9, 10
Stanley, Lady, 8, *9*
Stanley, Lord, 1, 4, 7–10
Stanowski, Wally, 103
Stevens, Julie, 122
sticks, *23*
Stimers, Rex, 108
Stirling, Jean, 94
Stratford Maids, 94
Stratford, Ontario, teams, 17
Sudbury team (1922), *72*
Sullivan, Ed, 125–26
Summerside P.E.I., Alpha women's team, 23
Summerside P.E.I., Crystal Sisters, 89, 91

Taylor, Billy, 103
Taylor, Fred "Cyclone," 56
Throop, Art, 40
timekeeper, 90
tobogganing, 50
Topp, Margaret, 97–98, *99*, 100–101
Toronto Aura Lee team, 64, 66, 83
Toronto Hockey League, 64, 66, 117
Toronto Humberside Dairy Queens, 124
Toronto Humberside Omegas, 129
Toronto Ladies Hockey League, 54, 55
Toronto Ladies team, 108
Toronto Litton's Canadettes, 130
Toronto Patterson Pats, 64, 66, 67, 68–70, 71, 82
Toronto Silverwoods, 83
Toronto Vagabonds, 87–88
Toronto Wellingtons, 34, 37
Tretiak, Vladislav, 158
Triance, Suzanne, 180
Tripp, Ada, 40
Tripp, Carla, 40–41
Trois–Rivières team, 16
trophies, 1, 7, 10, 58, 89, 90, 91, 144
TSN, 154
Tufford, Corwin Ray, 90–91
Tufford, Elenore, 90
Tufford, Rosemary, 90
Twiddy, Annabelle, 130

uniforms, *see* costumes
University of Guelph, 121, 192–95

University of Saskatchewan, 27, 58, 60, 115
University of Saskatchewan Tournament, 141
University of Toronto, 28, 32–33, 54–56, 63–64, 67, 84–85, 87, 115, 121, *129*, 179–80, 194–95
University of Western Ontario, 121

Vancouver teams, 13, 23
Varpalotai, Aniko, 148–49, 191
Varsity Arena, 55
Victoria Rink in Montreal, 51, *52*

Waghorne, Fred, 67
Walker, Hal, 127
Walker, Jean, 30, 32, 123
Walker, Mickey, 188–92, *193*
Wallaceburg Hornettes, 123
Wallaceburg Lipstick Tournament, 122–23
Walls, Miss, 26–27
Waterloo, Ontario, team, 34
Watson, Harry, 64
Western Inter–Varsity Athletic Union, 58
Westman, Mrs. Fran Crooks, 87–89
White, Edith, 24
Whitten, Erin, 2, 164, 186–87
Whitton, Charlotte, 56, *57*, 127
Wickenheiser, Hayley, 163, 164
Wilson, Bill, 115
Wilson, Stacy, *4*, 163, 166
Winnipeg Canadianettes, 114
Winnipeg Eatons, 91
Winnipeg Olympics (team), 97, 98, 100–101, 102, 103, 108
Women athletes, 45–49, 77–82, 116–19, 139, 201–202
Women's Collegiate Ice Hockey League, 58
Women's World Hockey Championships, 2, 87, 110, *136*, 138, *150*, 151–56, 159, 160–61, 162–66, 185, *200*
Women's World Hockey Championships, 1990 results, 164
Women's World Hockey Championships, 1992 results, 165
Women's World Hockey Championships, 1994 results, 165
World Women's Ice Hockey Tournament, 2, 143–49, 158
Wright, Sue, 132, 133
Wyatt, Miss, 86

Young, Scott, 122
Yuen, Susana, 152

Zeman, Joe, 26–27, 60, 90–91, 115